WORLD WAR 2 FOR TEENS – THE SECRET WAR

CODEBREAKERS, SPIES & RESISTANCE FIGHTERS. AMAZING FACTS, HEROES AND HOW THEY SHORTENED THE WAR

James Burrows

© Copyright 2025 - **All rights reserved.**

The content contained within this book may not be reproduced, duplicated or transmitted without direct written permission from the author or the publisher.

Under no circumstances will any blame or legal responsibility be held against the publisher, or author, for any damages, reparation, or monetary loss due to the information contained within this book, either directly or indirectly.

Legal Notice:

This book is copyright protected. It is only for personal use. You cannot amend, distribute, sell, use, quote or paraphrase any part, or the content within this book, without the consent of the author or publisher.

Disclaimer Notice:

Please note the information contained within this document is for educational and entertainment purposes only. All effort has been executed to present accurate, up to date, reliable, complete information. No warranties of any kind are declared or implied. Readers acknowledge that the author is not engaged in the rendering of legal, financial, medical or professional advice. The content within this book has been derived from various sources. Please consult a licensed professional before attempting any techniques outlined in this book.

By reading this document, the reader agrees that under no circumstances is the author responsible for any losses, direct or indirect, that are incurred as a result of the use of the information contained within this document, including, but not limited to, errors, omissions, or inaccuracies.

Other Books by James Burrows

What You Need To Know:

World War I for Teens
World War I for Kids
World War II for Teens
World War II for Kids
World War II for Teens – 21 Special Operations
World War II for Teens – The Secret War
The Vietnam War for Teens

The Ultimate Guide:

Egyptian Mythology for Kids
Greek Mythology for Kids
Norse Mythology for Kids

Other Books:

The Art of War – Sun Tzu
Meditations – Marcus Aurelius

CONTENTS

SPIES, SECRETS, AND THE FIGHT FOR FREEDOM

CODEBREAKERS

Chapter 1: Codebreaking – Staying One Step Ahead

Chapter 2: The Codebreakers' Headquarters

Chapter 3: Great Minds Don't Think Alike

Chapter 4: Heroes of Codebreaking

Chapter 5. How The Codes Were Broken

Chapter 6: Impact of Cracking Enigma and Purple

Chapter 7: The Moral Dilemma in Protecting the Enigma Secret

Chapter 8: A Crucial Contribution to The War Effort

SPIES

Chapter 1: Unsung Heroes of the Shadow War

Chapter 2: The Spy Organizations

- Britain's Special Operations Executive (SOE)
- The Office of Strategic Services (OSS)
- The Soviet Union's NKVD
- German Spy Agencies: Abwehr and Gestapo

- Japan's Spy Agencies: The Kempeitai and Tokumu Kikan

Chapter 3: Famous Spies and Their Stories

- Virginia Hall
- Noor Inayat Khan
- Juan Pujol (Garbo)
- Violette Szabo
- Duško Popov
- Johnny Jebsen
- Odette Sansom
- Fritz Kolbe
- Christine Granville
- Elvira de la Fuente Chaudoir
- Axis Spies

THE RESISTANCE

Chapter 1: The Resistance Fighters

Chapter 2: Resistance Movements in WW2

- The French Resistance
- The Polish Underground (Armia Krajowa)
- The Greek Resistance

- The Danish Resistance
- Yugoslav Partisans
- Czech Resistance
- The Chinese Resistance
- Filipino Guerrillas

Chapter 3: Heroes of the Resistance

- Jean Moulin
- Nancy Wake
- Lucie Aubrac
- Andrée De Jongh
- Georges Guingouin
- Henri Rol-Tanguy
- Joseph Epstein
- Sophie Scholl
- Witold Pilecki
- Le Chambon-sur-Lignon
- Elzbieta Zawacka

EPILOGUE: THE LEGACY OF ESPIONAGE, CODEBREAKING AND RESISTANCE IN WORLD WAR II

ABOUT THE AUTHOR

SPIES, SECRETS, AND THE FIGHT FOR FREEDOM

Have you ever imagined what it would be like to be a spy? Sneaking behind enemy lines, cracking secret codes, or delivering top-secret messages that could change the course of history? Sounds like something out of a movie, right? But during World War II, this wasn't Hollywood - it was real life.

Welcome to the world of spies, codebreakers, and resistance fighters, where danger was part of the job, and bravery wasn't optional. These people weren't just soldiers - they were ordinary men and women who did extraordinary things. Some worked in the shadows, gathering intelligence to outsmart the enemy. Others risked their lives helping those oppressed by the war, sabotaging enemy plans, or fighting back with whatever they could. Every act, no matter how small, helped bring an end to one of the darkest chapters in history.

Why were they so important? In the shadowy world of World War II, battles were not only fought with bullets and bombs but also with brains and brilliance. It was a game of strategy, and information was the ultimate weapon. Knowing what your enemy was planning - or keeping them in the dark about your own plans - could mean the difference between victory and defeat. That's where these hidden heroes came in. Their work helped shorten the war and saved countless lives.

But here's the thing – because so much of what they did was top secret, their stories often stayed hidden for decades. Now, we're peeling back the curtain to reveal some of the most daring, clever, and downright unbelievable missions you've probably never heard about.

In this book, you'll meet fearless spies who carried out dangerous missions, brilliant codebreakers who cracked "uncrackable" enemy codes, and courageous resistance fighters who stood against overwhelming odds. These weren't superheroes - they were regular people who stepped up when the world needed them most.

So, if you're ready for tales of suspense, danger, and heroism, let's dive in. These stories aren't just exciting—they remind us why it's so important to stand up for what's right and never forget those who risked it all for freedom. Get ready, because this is one adventure you'll never forget!

What Was WW2 All About

Let's take a quick step back and talk about the big picture – what World War II was all about and why it changed the world forever.

It all started in the late 1930s when the world was already struggling to recover from the Great Depression and the aftermath of World War I. Tensions were high, and some countries - like Germany, Italy, and Japan - wanted to expand their power and territories. In 1939, Germany, led by Adolf Hitler, invaded Poland, and that set off a chain reaction. Britain and France declared war on Germany, and soon the conflict spread across Europe and beyond.

The war was fought between two main groups: the Allies (including the United States, Britain, the Soviet Union, and many others) and the Axis powers (Germany, Italy, and Japan). It wasn't just about armies fighting on battlefields - this was a war that reached into cities, villages, and people's homes. Millions of innocent people, including entire families, were caught in the middle.

World War II lasted six years, from 1939 to 1945, and was filled with significant events. Germany's lightning-fast invasions in Europe, known as the "Blitzkrieg," seemed unstoppable at first. But then, the Allies began pushing back. Battles like Stalingrad and D-Day were crucial moments when the tide started to turn. Meanwhile, Japan attacked the United States at Pearl Harbor in 1941, dragging America into the fight.

The war finally ended in 1945 - Germany surrendered in May and Japan followed in September, after the U.S. dropped two atomic bombs. By then, the world was forever changed - millions of lives had been lost, cities had been destroyed, and countries had to rebuild.

World War II wasn't just a war of armies and tanks, but also about the tremendous bravery of individuals everywhere. From soldiers on the front lines to people fighting in secret, everyone had a role to play. And in this book, you're about to meet some of the most daring and inventive heroes of all: the spies, codebreakers, and resistance fighters who worked behind the scenes to help win the war.

Filled with incredible stories, you will find yourself in the middle of the Secret War, with those working in the shadows, using ingenuity to crack codes, courageous to resist the Nazis, and cunning to undermine the enemy.

Also, look out for these add-ons throughout the book with some incredible extra insights into the war:

❖ DID YOU KNOW

- *The U.S. Marines employed Navajo Native Americans to create an unbreakable code based on their language. This code played a crucial role in secure communications in the Pacific theater.*

- *Spy gadgets included bombs hidden in rats, messages in micro-dots, gun silencers, and shoes that left barefoot-looking footprints!*

Strap on your helmet, tighten your boots, and find out all you can about the Secret War!

CODEBREAKERS

CHAPTER 1: CODEBREAKING – STAYING ONE STEP AHEAD

While soldiers clashed on the front lines, another, quieter war raged behind closed doors - one fought in secret rooms filled with the hum of machines and the scratch of pencils on paper. This was the war of codebreaking.

Imagine what it would be like to create a message so perfectly encoded that no one could crack it. Now flip the scenario - working tirelessly, day and night, to unravel that message, desperate to uncover your enemy's plans before it's too late. During World War II, this wasn't just a challenge; it was a deadly game of hide-and-seek, where lives and nations hung in the balance.

The ability to intercept and decipher enemy communications became one of the most decisive factors in determining the course of the conflict. Every piece of broken code, every decrypted message, held the potential to save lives, redirect battles, and outmaneuver opponents.

Codebreaking wasn't just about understanding the enemy's plans; it was about staying one step ahead in a war where a single missed signal could spell disaster.

That's where the codebreakers stepped in. At Bletchley Park in England, brilliant minds turned the chaos of war into decipherable patterns, transforming vulnerability into strength. Their tools? Ingenuity, determination, and a deep understanding of cryptography - the art of creating and cracking secret codes.

In this chapter, we'll uncover the incredible story of WWII codebreaking. You'll learn about Germany's infamous Enigma machine and Japan's complex Purple Code - seemingly unbreakable systems that weren't as invincible as they thought. Meet the problem-solvers behind the breakthroughs, like mathematician Alan Turing, whose genius helped shorten the war and save lives.

The Importance of Codebreaking in WWII

In World War II, communication was everything. With millions of soldiers spread across continents and oceans, armies relied on constant updates to coordinate attacks, plan defenses, and stay one step ahead of the enemy. Orders had to be transmitted quickly and securely - whether it was a general sending a strategy to the front lines or a commander relaying acritical change of plans. Without communication, even the best-laid plans could fall apart.

Now imagine if you could listen in on the enemy's conversations. That's exactly what codebreaking teams were trying to do. By intercepting and decoding secret messages, they could uncover where troops were heading, where submarines were lurking, or when an attack was planned. This wasn't just about gaining an advantage - it could literally save lives. If you knew a bombing raid was coming, you could evacuate civilians or reposition defenses. If you cracked a code about an enemy convoy, you could reroute your ships to avoid an ambush or plan a counterattack.

Decoding messages could change the outcome of battles. For example, take the famous example of the Battle of Midway. U.S. codebreakers deciphered Japanese plans and thanks to the decrypted messages, the U.S. Navy knew the timing, composition, and objectives of the Japanese fleet. It turned what could have been a devastating loss into a major victory for the Allies. This wasn't luck - it was the result of tireless work by people who knew that every intercepted message could mean the difference between victory and defeat.

In short, communication wasn't just a tool in WWII - it was a weapon. And the ability to break the enemy's codes turned that weapon back on them, giving the Allies a powerful edge in a war where every decision counted.

Famous Encryption Systems

Germany's Enigma Machine

The German's Enigma machine was a ground breaking cipher device designed to encrypt and decrypt secret messages, making communication secure for its users. Originally invented by German engineer Arthur Scherbiusin the early 1920s, it was initially intended for commercial purposes. However, its true significance emerged when the German military adopted and enhanced it, using it extensively during World War II to protect their communications.

Enigma Machine, Bletchley Park

Lorenz Code

The Lorenz cipher system was used for secure communications between Nazi military and government high command. Unlike the Enigma machine, which was widely used for tactical messages, the Lorenz Cipher was used for strategic communications and conveyed critical plans, such as military strategies, troop deployments, and logistical details.

It was a sophisticated teleprinter encryption device. It worked by applying a complex cipher to plain text messages, turning them into ciphertext before transmission via radio.

Japan's Purple Code

The Japanese government was using an advanced cipher system to encrypt its most sensitive diplomatic communications. The Purple Code was the Allies' name for the encryption method used by Japan's Type B Cipher Machine, which was designed to secure messages exchanged between Japanese embassies and the foreign ministry.

CHAPTER 2: THE CODEBREAKERS' HEADQUARTERS

During World War II, codebreaking was more than simply great brains working alone; it was a vast collaborative effort. Thousands of individuals worked around the clock in secret places, breaking codes and intercepting enemy signals with the potential to affect the direction of the war. These clandestine centres, where the unseen battle of intelligence was fought, were spread across the globe. Let's have a look at some of the key areas where this work was done.

Bletchley Park (UK)

Bletchley Park, located in Buckinghamshire, England, was the central site for British codebreaking operations during World War II. This top-secret site became the focal point of Britain's cryptography operations and played a pivotal role in decrypting German and Axis communications, significantly contributing to the Allied war effort.

In 1938, as the threat of war grew, the British government purchased the Bletchley Park estate, recognizing the need for a central codebreaking hub. The site was chosen for its secluded location, proximity to London, and good railway links. It became the wartime headquarters of the Government Code and Cypher School (GC&CS) which had been established during World War I.

The goal was to intercept and decrypt enemy communications, particularly the complex Enigma and Lorenz ciphers used by German forces.

Bletchley Park

How Bletchley Park Worked

The site was divided into a series of "huts" to optimize the complex and highly secretive work of intercepting, decoding, and analyzing enemy communications. This organizational structure masterstroke of organization - by dividing the monumental task of codebreaking into manageable, specialized units, the Allies could harness the talents of a diverse workforce while maintaining strict security.

Functions of Key Huts:

- Hut 3: Responsible for translation and interpretation of decrypted German Army and Air Force messages.

- Hut 4: Focused on German Navy signals and provided intelligence reports.

- Hut 6: Dealt with decrypting German Army and Air Force Enigma messages.

- Hut 8: Led by Alan Turing, it concentrated on breaking German Naval Enigma, crucial for countering U-boat threats.

- Hut 11: Operated the Bombe machines, used to deduce Enigma settings.

- Hut 7: Specialized in Japanese naval codes, though most work on Japan was conducted elsewhere later in the war.

- Hut 14: Focused on disseminating Ultra intelligence to military leaders without revealing its source.

People working at Bletchley Park

Workflow Between Huts:

- Intercepted messages arrived at Bletchley Park from listening stations like Chicksands and Scarborough.

- Messages were first processed in huts responsible for decryption (e.g., Hut 6 or Hut 8) before being passed to huts like Hut 3 or Hut 4 for analysis and reporting.

- Intelligence summaries were sent to the War Office, Admiralty, or field commanders, often with strict controls on how the information could be used.

The division into huts allowed each team to focus on a specific task, such as decryption, translation, analysis, or intelligence dissemination. This specialization ensured that individuals with the right skills could concentrate on their areas of expertise without being distracted by unrelated work. The huts streamlined workflows, enabling simultaneous efforts on different aspects of codebreaking and intelligence processing. Tasks were clearly defined and organized in a pipeline, so decrypted data moved smoothly from one hut to the next.

Compartmentalization minimized the risk of sensitive information being leaked. Staff in one hut often knew little about what was happening in others, adhering to a strict "need-to-know" policy. This structure ensured that even if someone accidentally revealed information, the scope of the leak would be limited.

Decryption Process

- The decryption process began with intercepted signals sent to Bletchley Park from listening stations like those at Chicksands and Scarborough.

- Teams analyzed these signals, identifying patterns and weaknesses in enemy ciphers.

- Machines like the Bombe, developed by Alan Turing and Gordon Welchman, were used to automate and accelerate the breaking of Enigma codes.

- Later, the Colossus, the world's first programmable digital computer, was built to decipher Lorenz cipher messages used by high-level German command.

Collaboration

- Bletchley Park worked closely with allied codebreaking centers, such as Arlington Hall in the United States.

- Intelligence derived from Bletchley Park's work was codenamed Ultra and shared selectively with military leaders.

❖ **DID YOU KNOW**

- *The German battleship Bismarck was located with the assistance of Enigma decrypts and sunk by air and surface attack in 1941.*

Bletchley Park was a hub of activity from the start of the war. Here, some of Britain's best brains, including mathematicians, linguists, engineers, and puzzle lovers, gathered to decode enemy codes. To cope with the growing volume of work, the number of people working at Bletchley Park grew to over 9,000 by 1945. Maintaining absolute secrecy was vital. Workers were sworn to confidentiality, and Bletchley Park's existence remained classified until long after the war.

They toiled relentlessly, frequently in cramped rooms loaded with heaps of paper, charts, and devices. Recruits, many of whom were young women, worked in shifts around the clock, aware that their success or failure may influence the outcome of the war.

At its peak during World War II, Bletchley Park decoded, and processed around 5,000 messages a day. Breaking German ciphers required constant adaptation as the enemy improved its encryption methods.

Despite their diverse origins, everyone at Bletchley had one common goal: to break enemy codes. Bletchley Park was unique in that it brought individuals from all areas of life together, from academics and mathematicians to crossword solvers and military leaders. This varied team worked together seamlessly, with each individual's distinct abilities contributing to the achievement of their task.

❖ **DID YOU KNOW**

- *Staff working the night shift in Hut 6 were amongst the first people in the world to learn of the formal surrender of Germany in the early hours of*

May 7, 1945, gleaned from intercepted messages!

Arlington Hall (USA)

The United States was working diligently across the Atlantic, intercepting and deciphering German, and Japanese communications. The United States codebreaking secret headquarters, similar to Bletchley Park, was located at Arlington Hall, just outside Washington, D.C. Operated by the U.S. Army Signal Intelligence Service (SIS), it played a critical role in decrypting Japanese and Axis communications, complementing the work done at Bletchley Park. Arlington Hall was instrumental in breaking the Japanese diplomatic code known as Purple and contributed significantly to Allied intelligence.

Before the war, the Signal Intelligence Service (SIS), led by William Friedman, had already been working on breaking Japanese codes. As the war intensified, the U.S. needed a centralized, larger facility to manage the growing volume of intercepted enemy communications. Arlington Hall was selected in 1942 as the main headquarters for its codebreaking efforts, and with its proximity to Washington, D.C., it gave access to military and government offices while maintaining a level of secrecy.

Key Functions at Arlington Hall

1. Japanese Codebreaking

- Arlington Hall focused primarily on breaking Japanese diplomatic, military, and logistical codes. This included the Purple Code, a sophisticated cipher used by Japanese diplomats. Arlington Hall cryptanalysts, working with intelligence gleaned before the war, built a replica of Japan's Purple machine in 1940, enabling the Allies to intercept and read Japanese diplomatic messages. Army codes were broken, including messages about Japanese troop movements, particularly in the Pacific and China theaters, as well as breaking Japanese supply chain codes, enabling the Allies to disrupt operations and plan counterattacks.

2. Collaboration with Allies

- Arlington Hall worked closely with Bletchley Park and other Allied codebreaking centers, sharing decrypted intelligence through the BRUSA Agreement (British-U.S. collaboration on cryptanalysis).

- They also cooperated with Station HYPO in Hawaii, which focused on breaking Japanese naval codes like JN-25.

3. Intercepting Other Axis Communications

- Arlington Hall's work extended beyond Japan to decrypt messages from German and Italian sources, although the focus remained on Japan.

4. Cryptanalysis Techniques

- Cryptanalysts employed a combination of mathematical analysis, pattern recognition, and early computing devices to break complex codes. Manual labor was essential, with clerks and linguists processing vast amounts of intercepted messages.

At its peak, Arlington Hall employed over 10,000 people, including mathematicians, linguists, engineers, and clerical workers. Women made up a significant portion of the workforce, many recruited from college mathematics departments or secretarial roles. Notable figures included Genevieve Grotjan Feinstein, who made key contributions to breaking the Purple code.

Arlington Hall was organized into specialized teams focusing on different types of codes, regions, or languages. This division allowed for efficient processing and analysis of the vast quantities of intercepted communications.

Early computing machines like tabulating machines and punch card systems were used to analyze intercepted messages, and complemented manual decryption efforts and accelerated the process.

U.S. Army Signals Intelligence Service cryptologists at work at Arlington Hall

The Naval Communications Annex (USA)

The Naval Communications Annex (NCA) was established in 1942 after the attack on Pearl Harbor, and was a critical U.S. Navy cryptographic facility during World War II. Again, located in Washington, D.C., it served as the hub for breaking Japanese naval codes and coordinating communications intelligence (COMINT) for the U.S. Navy. The annex became home to OP-20-G, the U.S. Navy's cryptographic and signals intelligence branch. Its primary mission was to intercept, analyze, and decrypt Japanese naval codes, most notably JN-25, the main operational code used by the Imperial Japanese Navy (IJN).

Key Functions

1. Cryptanalysis of Japanese Naval Codes

- Breaking JN-25 code was a central part of the NCA's work. JN-25 was a complex cipher used for IJN operational and strategic communications, and analysts at the annex worked tirelessly to break it, providing critical intelligence for major battles. Decrypted JN-25 messages revealed Japanese plans for the Battle of Midway, enabling the U.S. to achieve a decisive victory.

- The annex also worked on other Japanese naval codes, including ship-to-ship communications and weather reports.

2. Collaboration with Field Units

- The Naval Communications Annex coordinated closely with field cryptographic units like Station HYPO in Hawaii and Station CAST in the Philippines. Intelligence was shared and analyzed jointly to create a comprehensive picture of Japanese naval operations.

3. Dissemination of Intelligence

- Deciphered communications were passed on to the Office of Naval Intelligence (ONI) and senior military leaders to inform strategic decisions.

4. Training and Research

- The annex also served as a training ground for cryptographers and researchers, ensuring a steady supply of skilled personnel for ongoing and future operations.

The annex employed a mix of military and civilian personnel, including many women, often recruited from colleges and universities for their mathematical and linguistic skills. Key figures included Commander Joseph Rochefort and Captain John Redman, who were instrumental in leading cryptographic efforts.

Work was divided into specialized teams focusing on different codes, languages, or regions, allowing for efficient processing of intercepted messages. Many of the personnel were women, often referred to as "Code Girls." They played vital roles in deciphering enemy codes and handling large volumes of intercepted communications.

Together with Bletchley Park, these two sites were essential to the Allies' WWII endeavours. American codebreakers, like the British cryptographers, were under tremendous pressure to decrypt signals before the enemy took action. Together, they were instrumental in obtaining information that altered the course of the war.

CHAPTER 3: GREAT MINDS DON'T THINK ALIKE

The variety of backgrounds among those who participated to the codebreaking operations during World War II was one of the most impressive features of the endeavour. Linguists, mathematicians, chess players, and even railway clerks were drawn to Bletchley Park and other encryption headquarters.

The adage "**Great minds think alike**" is well-known, but the intelligence services didn't want everyone to think the same - they wanted individuals with distinct viewpoints, abilities, and methods of problem-solving, individuals with photographic recalls or attention to detail, as well as individuals with a talent for solving puzzles, like crossword lovers, who were among the most unusual candidates.

The success of the codebreaking operation was partly due to the diverse set of abilities, backgrounds, and skills at Bletchley Park and other headquarters.

❖ **DID YOU KNOW**

- *Dilly Knox, who was well-known for his exceptional cryptanalysis abilities, had an unusual working style...he deciphered coded messages in the bathtub! Yes, to concentrate on cracking codes while unwinding in the water, he had a bathtub installed in his Bletchley Park office.*

- *Alan Turin had hayfever, so wore his gas mask when cycling in the countryside. The gas mask made him look odd, but it worked!*

Let's take a look at the type of people recruited to work at Bletchley Park.

Mathematicians: The Problem Solvers

Mathematicians formed the foundation of codebreaking at Bletchley Park. Their proficiency in reasoning, logic, problem-solving, and pattern recognition was crucial in deciphering intricate cyphers such as Lorenz and Enigma.

Linguists and Classicists: The Language Experts

Linguists and classicists were crucial in deciphering the codes. Fluent speakers of German, Italian, Japanese, and other Axis languages made up a large portion of the recruits at Bletchley Park. This was important because the codebreakers were able to decipher the encrypted data by knowing the language and context of the intercepted messages.

Professors and graduates from universities like Oxford and Cambridge, were highly regarded for their capacity to decipher not just difficult languages but also the subtleties and context of messages from the enemy.

Crossword Enthusiasts and Puzzle Solvers: The Creative Minds

People with sharp minds for solving puzzles were recruited for their ability to think creatively and spot patterns.

❖ DID YOU KNOW

- *Crossword enthusiasts were recruitment by novel means - through national puzzle competitions, including a well-known crossword challenge published in The Daily Telegraph!*

Engineers and Technicians: The Builders of Machines

Engineers and technicians were needed to construct and maintain the codebreaking machinery, while the mathematicians and linguists labored to decipher the codes. Codebreaking would have been a laborious, manual procedure in the absence of these devices. Two of the most significant codebreaking devices in history, the Bombe and the Colossus, were built with assistance from the engineers and technicians.

Women

Women made up nearly 75% of Bletchley Park's workforce, playing a vital, and often underappreciated, role in the war effort.

Woman working as cryptanalysts, such as Joan Clarke, were directly involved in breaking codes alongside their male counterparts. Clerical staff were needed for the labor-intensive tasks of organizing, analyzing, and transcribing intercepted enemy signals

Woman also worked as machine operators, controlling devices such as the Bombe and Colossus, ensuring the decryption process went smoothly and the equipment performed well.

Finally, woman worked as Intelligence Analysts. Following the decoding of the signals, intelligence analysts - many of whom were women - sought to interpret the data. They conducted an analysis of the intercepted signals and offered suggestions that influenced military tactics. Their efforts frequently resulted in choices that altered the direction of conflicts and the war's conclusion, assisting the Allies in winning.

Military Personnel

British military personnel were also instrumental in connecting the cryptanalysts' work to ongoing military activities. These military professionals ensured that critical intelligence was promptly turned into action by contributing invaluable technical knowledge and linguistic abilities. Military personnel ensured that intelligence gathered from codes was quickly passed along to the right people, helping shape military tactics and strategy on the front lines.

Academics and Scholars

Bletchley Park wasn't just a place for mathematicians and cryptanalysts—it was also home to academics and scholars from a wide range of fields. These men and women brought their intellectual rigor and problem-solving abilities to the task of cryptanalysis, helping break codes that seemed impossible to crack.

Their backgrounds included:

Philosophy: Many philosophers, known for their ability to think deeply and logically, were recruited to help solve cryptographic puzzles.

Physics: Some of the top physicists were brought in to assist with the complex mathematics involved in cracking codes like Enigma and Lorenz.

History: Historians' ability to analyze patterns and understand the context of messages helped them work with linguists to decrypt enemy communications.

Musicology: Surprisingly, some experts in music were recruited to Bletchley Park because of their skill in recognizing patterns in music - which translated well to recognizing patterns in encrypted codes.

Everyday People with Extraordinary Talent

While many of the individuals at Bletchley Park were highly trained in mathematics, linguistics, or other academic fields, some of the most valuable recruits came from unconventional backgrounds. They were ordinary people, with extraordinary talents, who were able to make a significant impact on codebreaking efforts despite not having formal training in cryptography.

These unusual recruits included:

Railway Clerks: A number of railway clerks were recruited for their exceptional ability to organize large amounts of data efficiently. This skill was essential for keeping track of intercepted messages, sorting them, and ensuring that important information was passed along to the codebreakers.

Postal Workers: Many postal workers, who had experience with organizing and routing communications, were recruited for their ability to manage vast amounts of incoming and outgoing intelligence. Their experience in dealing with large quantities of information was invaluable for maintaining order at Bletchley Park.

Photographic Memory and Attention to Detail: Some recruits had photographic memories, allowing them to remember huge volumes of information quickly. Others had a natural talent for paying attention to the smallest details, which proved to be an advantage in spotting subtle patterns in enemy communications.

Despite the wide variety of backgrounds and skills at Bletchley Park, there were a few things that all the recruits had in common.

Discretion: All Bletchley Park staff were sworn to secrecy, and their work remained classified for many decades after the war. They knew that the success of their mission depended on their ability to keep their work under wraps, and they carried this responsibility with utmost seriousness.

Dedication: The pressure at Bletchley Park was intense, with long hours and life-or-death stakes. But every recruit was deeply dedicated to the cause. They worked tirelessly, knowing that their efforts could help save lives and change the outcome of the war.

Teamwork: Perhaps the most important quality that defined the work at Bletchley Park was teamwork. Mathematicians, linguists, engineers, and everyday workers all collaborated closely to break the codes. No one person could have done it alone. Their ability to work together, share ideas, and support each other was the key to their success.

By bringing together this diverse group of people - each with their own set of skills, experiences, and backgrounds - Bletchley Park became a hub of innovation and ingenuity. Together, these ordinary individuals helped change the course of history and profoundly influenced the outcome of World War II.

CHAPTER 4: HEROES OF CODEBREAKING

Every codebreaking achievement has a hero at its core. Despite working in secret and sometimes going unnoticed throughout their lifetimes, these men and women made contributions that altered the outcome of World War II. The heroes of codebreaking come from a variety of backgrounds, including linguists, mathematicians, cryptanalysts, and military leaders. Let's get to know some of the bright minds that contributed to the Allies' success by helping to uncover the enemy's secrets.

Alan Turing

Alan Turing is one of the most well-known individuals in the history of codebreaking and is often referred to as the "father of modern computing." A crucial person at Bletchley Park, Turing was a mathematician and logician who helped crack the German Enigma code, which the Nazis used to encrypt their military communications.

In 1936, Turing published his seminal paper, "On Computable Numbers, with an Application to the Entscheidungsproblem" (Decision Problem). This paper introduced the concept of the Turing Machine, a theoretical device capable of simulating any algorithm. It became the foundation of modern computer science.

Alan Turing

Turing earned his PhD at Princeton University where he also worked on cryptographic systems, including secure voice encryption devices, hinting at his later interest in cryptography.

Turing returned to Cambridge in 1938 and resumed his fellowship at King's College. He also began part-time work with the GC&CS, Britain's intelligence organization, focusing on cryptography. This involvement with GC&CS introduced him to the challenge of breaking the Enigma code, a task that would dominate his time at Bletchley Park.

He was a visionary thinker. Turing's groundbreaking concept of the Turing Machine anticipated modern computing. His ability to envision solutions far ahead of his time allowed him to see how machines could automate complex processes like codebreaking.

Turing possessed an extraordinary ability to combine theoretical mathematics with practical problem-solving. His statistical innovations and logical methods revolutionized cryptanalysis.

Despite immense pressure and frequent setbacks, Turing persisted in his efforts, driven by a deep sense of duty to defeat the Axis powers.

He approached problems unconventionally, seeing patterns and connections that others missed. Turing's genius was not limited to his intelligence; he also created the Bombe, a device that automatically decoded messages encrypted using Enigma. Decoding these communications was a laborious, manual procedure prior to the Bombe. However, Turing's invention greatly accelerated the process, and this technological advancement is credited with helping the Allies decipher German codes so successfully.

In addition to helping the Allies win battles, Turing's work is credited with saving millions of lives and cutting the war short by two to four years.

After the war, Turing turned his focus to computing, designing one of the first stored-program computers, the Automatic Computing Engine (ACE).

He also laid the groundwork for artificial intelligence, posing the question, "Can machines think?" and proposing the Turing Test, still used as a benchmark for AI.

Though his wartime achievements remained secret for many decades, Turing is now recognised as one of the 20th century's brightest thinkers, a visionary whose work continues to shape the world.

Turing's life met a tragic end in spite of his vital contribution to the military effort. Despite his unparalleled contributions, Turing faced severe prejudice due to his homosexuality, which was illegal in Britain at the time. In 1952, he was convicted and subjected to chemical castration. The persecution he endured likely contributed to his untimely death in 1954, widely believed to be a suicide.

The British government formally apologized for his mistreatment in 2009, and he was posthumously pardoned in 2013.

❖ *DID YOU KNOW*

- *Alan Turin invented the first computerized chess game!*

- *He was an Olympic level runner, finishing just 11 minutes short of the Olympic marathon runner at a qualifying event in 1948. Turing would occasionally run the 40-mile stretch between London and Bletchley Park for meetings! He said "I have such a stressful job that the only way I can get it out of my mind is by running hard."*

Emily Anderson

Emily Anderson was a remarkable Irish linguist and codebreaker whose expertise in languages, including German, Italian, and French, played a key role in the Allied codebreaking efforts during World War II, where she was a trailblazer in intelligence.

She pursued a career in academia, becoming a professor at the age of 26. However, she gave up her academic post, when she was one of the first women recruited to British Intelligence, in 1918, working at the newly formed Government Code & Cipher Code (now known as GCHQ). She was no wallflower too – she demanded equal pay and grading to the men – something very unusual in those days!

British Intelligence was looking for someone who could look at a sheet of paper containing a mix of words and numbers, and figure out what language it was in, what was being said and if this code would last before it was changed, and they'd have to start again. In World War 2, her linguistic skills were vital in decrypting Axis military communications, especially in translating and interpreting German messages. Her linguistic precision and deep understanding of German culture made her indispensable in interpreting nuanced military communications. Her knowledge of German military terminology and tactics enhanced the accuracy of intelligence reports. She also contributed to the deciphering of Enigma machine messages, enabling the Allies to anticipate and counter German strategies.

In 1940, she requested to be closer to the point where Italian signals were intercepted, so she could decrypt them faster. She was posted to Cairo where she setup cipher department.

Emily's work often involved collaborating with cryptanalysts, mathematicians, and intelligence officers to turn decrypted messages into actionable intelligence for the war effort.

She returned to London in 1943 and stayed with GC&CS until 1950. She resumed her academic pursuits, becoming a respected authority on German literature and music. She is particularly renowned for her translations of Mozart's letters, which remain an important resource in musicology today.

Like many others, she never spoke to anyone about what she'd done in the war!

Gordon Welchman

At Bletchley Park, mathematician and cryptanalyst Gordon Welchman collaborated closely with Alan Turing. He played a key role in enhancing Turing's Bombe machine, which was used to crack the Enigma code. Welchman's changes improved the Bombe's efficiency and greatly accelerated the decryption of encrypted messages.

In addition, Welchman was instrumental in cracking the German Luftwaffe (Air Force) codes, which were vital for Allied operations, particularly during the Battle of the Atlantic. He was one of the key players in the Ultra intelligence operation that helped change the course of the war because of his ability to develop devices that disrupted top-level military communications.

Joan Clarke

One of the few women at Bletchley Park who collaborated closely with Alan Turing to crack the Enigma code was Joan Clarke. Clarke was one of the few females in a male-dominated field, yet she excelled as a mathematician and cryptanalyst.

She studied cipher texts punched out in long sheets of alphabetical columns to work out the probable right and middle rotor starting positions on the Enigma machine. Her work contributed significantly to breaking the Enigma codes.

Because of how essential her contributions were, she was given the opportunity to serve as Turing's deputy, a post often held by males. Within the cryptography field, Clarke was well respected for her brilliance and tenacity.

After the war, Clarke joined the British Government Communications Head Quarters (GCHQ). She worked in H division on the 'Vanona' project, decoding communications sent between Soviet agents. She finally left GCHQ in 1982!

Her contributions were not properly recognised until much later, though, as her work was kept under wraps for decades like that of many of her colleagues.

❖ **DID YOU KNOW**

- *Clarke was engaged to Turing in the spring of 1941: their families were informed, but it was kept secret from their colleagues. Turing later broke off the engagement.*

Hugh Alexander

Another top cryptanalyst at Bletchley Park, Hugh Alexander is renowned for his contributions to the deciphering of the German Lorenz and Enigma cyphers. The success of Ultra, the top-secret intelligence program that gave the Allies vital knowledge about the enemy's plans and movements, was largely due to Alexander's work.

Alexander's efforts directly aided in the preparation of the 1944 Allied invasion of Normandy, known as D-Day. In the critical days preceding the invasion, his ability to crack the Lorenz codes gave the Allies a tactical edge that allowed them to execute the operation with few surprises from the Axis troops.

Mavis Batey

One of the most significant female codebreakers at Bletchley Park, Mavis Batey worked on cracking the German Enigma and the Italian Naval cypher. By successfully deciphering the Italian code, Batey's team was able to intercept vital Axis messages. Battles in the Mediterranean were won thanks in large part to this intelligence.

In addition to cracking codes, Batey's efforts were essential in giving the Allies the useful intelligence they required to outmanoeuvre the Axis troops. Like many others, Batey never discussed her work in public until much later in life, despite the importance of her contributions.

William Friedman

William Friedman, was instrumental in cracking Japan's codes, especially the Purple cypher. The United States was able to translate high-level Japanese messages, including those from Emperor Hirohito and other high-ranking officials, thanks to Friedman's work at the U.S. Army Signal Intelligence Service (SIS). A number of significant successes in the Pacific, notably the pivotal Battle of Midway, were made possible by the successful cracking of these codes.

Dilly Knox

Dilly Know started his codebreaking career in World War I. During World War 2 he led the team that made the first wartime breaks into German Enigma, broke the Italian Naval Enigma machine in 1940 which led to the Allied victory at the naval battle of Cape Matapan off Greece, and the Abwehr version in 1942.

He led the meetings with the Poles and French on the eve of the war which disclosed Polish understanding of the Enigma system.

By the end of the war, his unit had decrypted 140,800 messages!

Marian Rejewski

Marian Rejewski was the first person to crack the Enigma code, in just ten weeks. His excellent mathematical education, fluent command of German, exceptional intuition and completion of a course in cryptology, together with the intelligence information he received from the French Secret Service, led to his success. The first messages were deciphered as early as Christmas 1932.

Marian Rejewski

In 1938 the German cryptographers increased Enigma's security and the Poles' techniques no longer worked.

With war imminent, the Poles invited French and British code breakers for a secret meeting near Warsaw. The Polish team disclosed their Enigma results and handed their allies-to-be copies of the Enigma machine. On 1 September the war broke out. The three genius mathematicians fled Poland and later joined the

French cryptographers in France. The knowledge they had provided considerably contributed to the cracking of the more complicated wartime Enigma codes used by the Germans.

Bill Tutte

Bill Tutte, and his colleagues, worked on cracking the Lorez code. His work is considered one of the greatest intellectual achievements of World War 2!

He was given an almost impossible task at Bletchley Park – to decipher codes that were being sent on a new teletype system, the Lorenz system, without ever seeing the device that produced the complicated codes (Bletchley Park only obtained a Lorenz machine after the war ended!).

Tutte constructed a model of that device and then created algorithms to crack its codes. It allowed the British to access Hitler's most secret communications – high level, strategic communication – contributed greatly to the shortening of the war. and led to the early development of the modern computer.

CHAPTER 5: HOW THE CODES WERE BROKEN

Germany's Enigma Machine

The German's Enigma machine was a groundbreaking cipher device designed to encrypt and decrypt secret messages, making communication secure for its users. Originally invented by German engineer Arthur Scherbius in 1918, it was initially intended for commercial purposes, to transmit secure messages. Scherbius aimed to provide businesses and governments with a reliable way to protect sensitive information, particularly in the aftermath of World War I, when secure communication was increasingly vital.

However, its true significance emerged when the German military adopted and enhanced it in the late 1920s. The Reichsmarine (German Navy) first adopted Enigma in 1926, followed by the Reichswehr (Army) in 1928.

The military versions included enhancements, such as additional rotors and a plugboard, which significantly increased the encryption's complexity.

By the time of World War II, the Enigma machine was used across all branches of the German military, including the Army, Navy, and Luftwaffe. Its flexibility and portability made it an ideal tool for field communication.

What It Was Used For

The Enigma machine was primarily used by the German armed forces to send and receive coded messages, ensuring that crucial orders and plans remained secure. It was deployed across various branches, including the navy, air force, and army, and even in diplomatic communications.

How Did The Enigma Machine Work?

The Enigma's strength came from its staggering number of possible configurations. Each machine had a set of rotors, each with 26 possible positions corresponding to the letters of the alphabet. Operators could arrange these rotors in different orders, and a plugboard allowed pairs of letters to be swapped, further increasing the complexity. The rotors were the heart of the Enigma machine, with each keystroke advancing the rotor mechanism and changing the cipher, making it extremely difficult to crack without knowing the initial settings.

Operators would input a plain text message, and the machine would output an encrypted version. The recipient, using the same settings, could decrypt the message.

When all settings were combined, the Enigma machine had an astronomical 150,000,000,000,000,000,000 (150 quintillion) possible combinations! This made it seem practically unbreakable, even with meticulous efforts.

Why Was It So Difficult to Crack?

1. Daily Key Changes: The settings on the Enigma were changed daily, meaning even if a code was broken one day, the solution wouldn't work the next.

2. Dynamic Encryption: Each time a letter was pressed, the rotors would shift, creating a new encryption for every letter in a message. This dynamic nature meant patterns were extremely difficult to detect.

3. Plugboard Customization: The plugboard (or steckerbrett) added another layer of encryption by swapping pairs of letters before and after the rotor encryption, further scrambling the output.

4. Operator Variability: Human operators using different initial settings and combinations introduced variability, making it even harder to predict or replicate the machine's output.

The Enigma's complexity convinced the Germans it was unbreakable, leading them to use it for countless critical communications. However, as we will see, the British, led by outstanding mathematical brains like Alan Turing, devised ingenious methods and machines to crack its codes, gaining access to German secret communications, especially in the Battle of the Atlantic, helping to turn the tide of war in the Allies' favor.

Early Efforts to Break Enigma

In the 1930s, Polish mathematicians, led by Marian Rejewski, developed techniques to break early versions of the Enigma machine. They built a device called the bomba kryptologiczna (cryptologic bomb) to automate decryption. In 1939, the Poles shared their findings with the British and French, laying the groundwork for later breakthroughs at Bletchley Park.

How Was It Finally Broken

The breaking of the Enigma code by Alan Turing and other codebreakers working with him, was one of the greatest British coups of the Second World War. It helped ships delivering vital supplies to the UK during the darkest days of the war to evade the packs of German U-boats trying to hunt them down. This enabled Britain to rebuild its strength and re-equip its armies in preparation for its bid to expel the Nazi armies from Europe. The difference was substantial; in June 1941 Allied shipping losses were 432,000 tons, by August it was less than 80,000 tons

Alan Turing began work on breaking the German Enigma cipher shortly after joining Bletchley Park in September 1939.

Upon arrival, Turing joined the Hut 8 team, responsible for decrypting German naval communications. He quickly began developing a conceptual framework for attacking the Enigma machine, focusing on exploiting predictable features in German message settings, such as repeated message keys and common phrases (e.g., "Heil Hitler").

Turing's most significant contribution was the design of the Bombe (1939–1940), an automated tool to find the correct Enigma rotor settings (the daily key) used for encryption (The Bombe was not a codebreaker by itself).

He worked with Gordon Welchman, who introduced the diagonal board, which improved the Bombe's efficiency by cross-referencing additional logical connections in the cipher, speeding up the elimination of incorrect configurations.

Bombe at Bletchley Park

To decrypt a message, the Allies needed to know the rotor order and their settings (positions of each rotor and their ring settings) and the plugboard settings, which introduced additional letter substitutions. Enigma's design allowed for trillions of possible combinations, making brute-force decryption impossible by hand. However, messages often contained predictable phrases or cribs (e.g., weather reports, common salutations). If a portion of plaintext could be guessed, it created a starting point for testing possible rotor configurations.

How the Bombe Worked

Cryptanalysts would input a crib (common phrases or predictable text fragments) and align it with the ciphertext. This alignment created a logical map of how letters should substitute each other. The Bombe simulated multiple Enigma machines running in parallel. It systematically tested rotor settings that could produce the observed substitutions.

The Bombe's central mechanism was a series of rotating drums that mimicked the rotors of the Enigma machine. Each set of drums represented a possible rotor configuration. The machine used logical circuits to determine whether a given configuration could explain the crib-ciphertext relationship.

To eliminate impossibilities, the Bombe used a process called mechanical elimination. If a configuration didn't fit the logical constraints of the Enigma (e.g., a letter substituting for itself), it was ruled out. This dramatically reduced the number of possibilities that cryptanalysts needed to test manually.

The Bombe stopped when it found a potential solution—a rotor configuration that didn't violate any constraints. Cryptanalysts then tested this configuration on a real Enigma machine to see if it fully decrypted the message.

By automating much of the decryption process, the Bombe allowed cryptanalysts to test thousands of configurations far faster than manual efforts.

The first breakthroughs in deciphering Enigma messages began within a few months of Turing's arrival at Bletchley with the first operational Bombe, named "Victory". It was delivered to Bletchley Park in March 1940, and production ramped up afterward.

Kriegsmarine Version

The Kriegsmarine (German Navy) used a more complex version of the Enigma machine, presenting a greater challenge than the versions used by the army and air force.

In May 1941, the British captured key cryptographic materials, from the German weather ship Munchen and the U-boat U-110. The capture included an operational Enigma machine, including its rotors, and, most importantly, codebooks containing key settings and cipher tables. These codebooks were crucial because they allowed Allied cryptographers to reconstruct the German naval cipher system.

The seizing of the Enigma machine was kept secret - Commander Baker-Cresswell realised it was imperative that the Germans didn't know it had fallen in British hands as they would have changed the codes. The crew of the U-Boat were led to believe it had sunk before the boarding party arrived.

Before this event, British cryptographers at Bletchley Park had limited success in breaking the Kriegsmarine (German Navy) Enigma cipher. Naval communications were more complex and secure than those of the German Army or Air Force. The U-110 codebooks provided the critical keys to break the naval Enigma cipher, codenamed "Shark".

These captures, combined with Turing's Bombe, allowed the Allies to begin regularly decrypting German naval messages by mid-1941.

Security Changes and Blackout

The work continued throughout the war as the Germans introduced new security measures, such as those in 1942, requiring constant adaptation by Turing and his colleagues. These changes included adding a 4th rotor, changing key settings daily, and introducing stricter communication protocols.

These changes were driven by the Germans' increasing awareness of the possibility of cryptographic vulnerability, even though they underestimated the extent of Allied codebreaking efforts.

These changes created a significant setback for the Allies - from February to December 1942, the Allies were unable to read German naval Enigma messages effectively, leading to a period known as the "Blackout" in the Atlantic. In this time, hundreds of thousands of tons of allied shipping was sunk each month. There was a growing fear that Britain might eventually be starved into submission. However, this all changed on October 30, 1942, when the U-boat, U-559, was seized.

U-559, commanded by Kapitänleutnant Hans Heidtmann, was detected and pursued by Allied forces, including the destroyers HMS Petard, HMS Pakenham, and other naval vessels. After a prolonged hunt, the U-boat was depth-charged, forcing it to surface in the Mediterranean Sea, near Port Said, Egypt.

As U-559's crew began abandoning the submarine, they attempted to scuttle it by opening the sea cocks to flood the vessel, intending to prevent its secrets from falling into Allied hands. A British boarding party, including sailors Colin Grazier and Tony Fasson, along with a young canteen assistant, Tommy Brown (who was just 16 years old), swam to the sinking U-boat to retrieve vital materials.

Inside the U-boat, Fasson and Grazier located codebooks, charts, and Enigma keying materials, including the crucial short signal codebook (Kurzsignalheft) and weather codebook. They passed these items to Brown, who carried them to safety on HMS Petard. Unfortunately, the flooding submarine sank before Fasson and Grazier could escape, and both men were lost.

The U-559 operation was a pivotal moment in the Battle of the Atlantic. The retrieved codebooks provided vital information about German Kriegsmarine Enigma procedures, particularly for U-boat communications. These materials allowed cryptographers at Bletchley Park to once again break German naval Enigma traffic, and discover U-boat movements in the Atlantic and Mediterranean.

❖ **DID YOU KNOW**

- *When they abandoned ship, the Germans had forgotten to destroy their codebooks – the text was printed on water soluble ink, so the books simply needed to be immersed in water!*

- *Colin Grazier and Tony Fasson were posthumously awarded the George Cross for their heroism. Tommy Brown, who survived the war, received the George Medal for his role in the operation.*

The Lorenz Cipher

The Lorenz cipher, also known by the British codename Tunny, was a highly complex encryption system used by the German military during World War II for transmitting strategic, high-level communications. It was distinct from the Enigma machine, which was used for more tactical and field-level messages.

Lorenz SZ42 teleprinter attachment cipher machine

What Was the Lorenz Cipher Used For?

The Lorenz cipher encrypted messages sent via teletype machines (teleprinters) rather than Morse code. It was used for long-distance communication between German High Command and field generals, conveying critical plans, orders, and intelligence.

Employed by the Wehrmacht (German Army) and Luftwaffe, the Lorenz cipher was reserved for highly confidential and sensitive messages.

How It Worked

The encryption was achieved through the Lorenz SZ40/42 cipher machine, which used a series of twelve rotors to generate a pseudo-random binary stream that encrypted plaintext into cipher text. Messages were transmitted as streams of encoded characters, making them suitable for rapid communication over long distances.

Was Lorenz More Difficult to Crack Than Enigma

The Lorenz cipher was significantly more complex than Enigma, making it harder to break.

Key Differences:

1. Complexity:

- Lorenz used 12 wheels (compared to Enigma's 3 or 4 rotors) with varying numbers of pins, creating an astronomical number of possible settings.
- The encryption process involved binary addition (XOR logic) of plaintext and key streams, rather than the substitution cipher used by Enigma.

2. Volume of Data:

- Lorenz messages were often thousands of characters long, compared to shorter Enigma messages. The larger size of Lorenz transmissions made cryptanalysis more daunting but also provided more data for analysis.

3. Security:

- Lorenz messages were more tightly controlled, with fewer procedural errors (e.g., message key repetitions) compared to Enigma. These errors in Enigma operations often provided footholds for codebreakers.

Lorenz's complexity required advanced mathematical and logical reasoning, far exceeding the methods used for Enigma.

The scale of computation needed for breaking Lorenz was unprecedented, prompting innovations like Colossus, which could process thousands of characters per second to identify patterns.

How It Was Broken

The key to breaking the Lorenz cipher was to deduce the wheel settings used for encryption. These settings determined how the cipher transformed plaintext into ciphertext. Patterns needed to be broken which could then statistically infer the wheel positions—a labor-intensive and time-sensitive task if done manually.

The breakthrough came partly from human error! In August 1941, German operators retransmitted a long Lorenz-encrypted message with only slight changes to the settings, inadvertently giving cryptanalysts at Bletchley Park crucial insights into how Lorenz encryption worked.

Using the intercepted messages and known plaintext, cryptanalysts like Bill Tutte deduced the structure of the Lorenz machine without ever seeing one.

Tutte's work formed the basis for automated decryption efforts, leading to the development of Colossus, the world's first programmable digital computer.

How Colossus Helped

Colossus was a large, room-sized computer built using vacuum tubes (valves), which allowed it to process data much faster than electromechanical devices like the Bombe used for Enigma.

It was a specialized machine designed to perform complex statistical and logical operations, essential for analyzing intercepted Lorenz-encrypted messages.

The first Colossus machine became operational in February 1944, with later improved versions (like Colossus Mark II) increasing speed and capabilities.

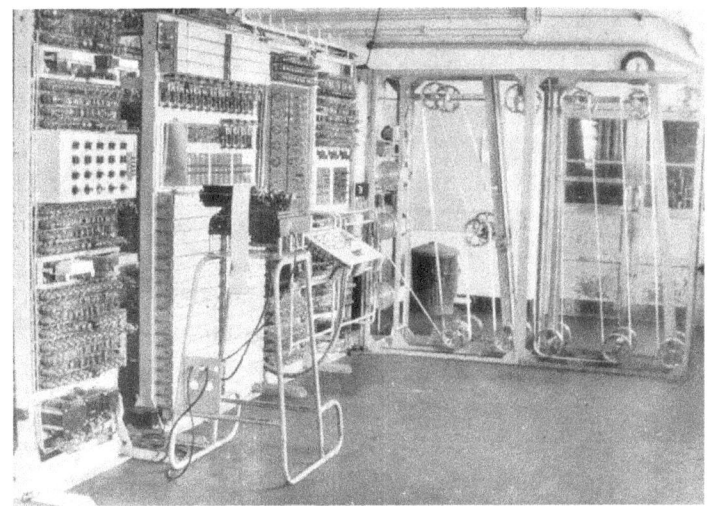

Colossus 10 in Block H, Bletchley Park

Colossus focused on 3 areas:

- **Pattern Matching:** It was designed to rapidly process intercepted ciphertext and search for repeating patterns.

- **Statistical Analysis:** It performed high-speed comparisons between possible key streams and the intercepted ciphertext, testing millions of possible configurations far faster than humans could.

- **Automating Decryption:** By automating the trial-and-error process of testing wheel positions, Colossus dramatically reduced the time needed to decode messages. It could perform 5,000 logical operations per second, a ground breaking achievement for the time! This allowed cryptanalysts to process large volumes of data quickly.

The Germans were completely unaware that the British had cracked the Lorenz cipher. Unlike the Enigma machine, which the Germans suspected might have been compromised due to various procedural breaches, the secrecy surrounding the cracking of Lorenz was so effective that they remained oblivious to the security breach.

This secrecy was helped by the fact that the Lorenz cipher had been broken without ever capturing a Lorenz machine during the war, leaving no evidence to alert the Germans. Lorenz cipher operators were typically more disciplined than those using Enigma, but the mistake in in August 1941 enabled British codebreakers to reverse-engineer the Lorenz machine. The Germans likely dismissed this as an isolated incident and did not investigate its consequences.

The Allies' use of Colossus was so advanced that it operated far beyond what the Germans imagined possible. The Germans likely assumed their cipher's complexity made it unbreakable.

The British were extremely careful to conceal their success with Lorenz. Intelligence derived from the cipher, known as "Ultra" intelligence, was used cautiously, ensuring it did not arouse suspicion. To disguise the source of information, the British often attributed their insights to spies, aerial reconnaissance, or other intelligence channels, a practice called "sanitization."

Even after the war, the Germans were shocked to learn that Lorenz had been compromised. The secrecy surrounding the Lorenz cipher-breaking effort was so complete that details about how it was achieved remained classified for decades. Only in the late 20th century did the full story of Bletchley Park, Bill Tutte, and Colossus come to light.

The ability to read high-level German communications provided the Allies with invaluable insights into German strategies and plans, particularly on the Eastern Front and in relation to D-Day. The Germans' ignorance of the breach allowed the Allies to maintain their strategic advantage until the very end of the war.

❖ **DID YOU KNOW**

- *The British used an encryption machine called TypeX, based on the commercially available Enigma machines but with a few changes to make the cipher more secure. A TypeX machine without rotors was captured by German forces at Dunkirk during the Battle of France and the Germans tried to crack it. However, the B-Dienst codebreaking organisation gave up on it after six weeks, when further time and personnel for such attempts were refused!*

TypeX cipher machine

Japan's Purple Code

The Japanese government was using an advanced cipher system to encrypt its most sensitive diplomatic communications. The Purple Code was the Allies' name for the encryption method used by Japan's Type B Cipher Machine. It was primarily used for diplomatic communications, not military ones. Messages encrypted with Purple often contained vital information about Japan's foreign policy, negotiations, and strategic intentions.

What Made Purple Special?

Unlike simpler codes or ciphers, Purple used a machine-based system with electromechanical stepping switches to scramble messages. This made it more advanced than older manual systems and similar in principle to Germany's Enigma machine, though its design was entirely different.

Why Was It Called "Purple"?

The Allies named the Japanese cipher systems using colors for classification. "Red" was an earlier Japanese code, and when they encountered the more advanced Type B machine, it was designated Purple, a step up in complexity.

How Did It Work?

Purple messages were encrypted by replacing characters based on an intricate system of substitutions. The machine divided the Japanese kana syllabary and Latin letters into two groups, creating complex substitutions that varied with every use. This complexity was designed to make interception and decryption nearly impossible without the machine itself.

How Was Purple Broken?

Despite its sophistication, Purple was cracked by U.S. cryptographers in 1940, before the U.S. even entered World War II.

U.S. intelligence intercepted encrypted diplomatic communications between Japanese embassies. Cryptanalysts, including a brilliant team at the U.S. Army's Signal Intelligence Service (SIS) led by William Friedman, studied the intercepted messages for patterns. Without ever seeing the actual Purple machine, the cryptanalysts reverse-engineered it. Using electromechanical components, they constructed a working replica that allowed them to decrypt Japanese messages in real time.

Why Was This Important?

Breaking Purple provided the Allies with critical insights into Japan's diplomatic intentions and strategies. For example, communications provided details on Japan's negotiations with Germany and Italy, including their role in the Tripartite Pact, forming the Axis alliance. The messages also included warnings about Pearl Harbor, which were misinterpreted. Messages decrypted in late 1941 indicated that Japan was preparing for war and that diplomatic efforts with the United States were likely to fail. Although Purple decrypts didn't explicitly reveal the Pearl Harbor attack, they highlighted heightened Japanese urgency and growing hostility.

Though Purple was a diplomatic code and not a military one, the intelligence gained from breaking it gave the Allies gained information about troop movements, supply chains, and strategic priorities.

Japan's JN-25 Naval Codes

The Japanese also has secret naval codes, called JN-25. This was used to coordinate fleet movements and military operations. Breaking JN-25 gave the U.S. crucial details about Japanese military strategies, including the attack plans for Midway.

U.S. cryptanalysts at Station HYPO in Hawaii, led by Commander Joseph Rochefort, cracked parts of JN-25 in the months leading up to the Battle of Midway. By doing so, they uncovered Japan's plan to attack a location they referred to as "AF". They also discovered the timing and composition of the Japanese fleet, allowing Admiral Chester Nimitz to set up an ambush.

This intelligence led to the American victory at Midway, turning the tide of the war in the Pacific, as we will discover in the next chapter.

CHAPTER 6: IMPACT OF CRACKING ENIGMA AND PURPLE

The Battle of the Atlantic

Breaking the Enigma cipher had a profound and specific impact on the Battle of the Atlantic, a critical theater in World War II where the Allies sought to secure vital supply lines across the Atlantic Ocean while German U-boats aimed to disrupt them.

With the interceptions and decrypted Enigma messages detailing U-boat positions, operational orders, and areas of patrol, Allied Atlantic convoys could be re-routed away from concentrations of U-Boats, significantly reducing loss of merchant ships carrying troops, weapons, supplies, and crucially, food.

Allies were able to better target 6this naval and air assets to hunt down and destroy U-Boats, reducing the overall effectiveness of the whole U-Boat fleet. As U-boat losses mounted and their effectiveness declined, the Germans diverted resources to shore up defenses and adapt tactics, weakening their overall naval campaign. One notable example was the sinking of U-boats attempting to refuel or resupply from supply ships known as "milk cows," which Enigma intelligence revealed.

By mid-1943, the tide had turned decisively in the Allies' favor, ensuring the steady flow of supplies critical to sustaining the fight against the Axis powers The U-boat menace was no longer the existential threat it had been in the early years of the war

D-Day Preparations

In its planning for D-Day, the Allies were able to gain critical insights into German defenses, troop deployments, and strategic thinking, through its Ultra intelligence, giving them Allies a decisive advantage.

It helped the Allies better understand German defenses, including orders about fortifications in the Atlantic Wall, the extensive coastal defenses designed to repel an invasion, showing where defenses were weakest and strongest. This helped persuade the Allies to select Normandy as the invasion site over other options like Pas de Calais, which was more heavily defended.

In the build up to the D-Day invasion, the Allies ran a huge deception campaign, called Operation Fortitude, designed to fool the Germans into thinking the Allies would invade France at Calais. By reading German messages, the Allies confirmed that the Germans believed all the false information they were being fed, and that they thought the invasion would occur at Pas de Calais, keeping German forces distracted and away from Normandy. As a result, fewer German reinforcements were available to counter the actual landings.

German troop movements were also tracked, revealing the positioning of German divisions, particularly the 15th Army stationed at Pas de Calais and the movement of panzer divisions in France. This enabled the Allies to plan the timing and scale of the invasion to avoid the largest concentrations of German forces. Ultra intercepts highlighted delays in German Panzer reinforcements due to confusion over whether the actual invasion was a feint. This gave the Allies valuable time to establish a beachhead.

German communications about the effectiveness of Allied bombing campaigns on transportation and supply routes confirmed that these pre-invasion efforts were succeeding in disrupting German logistics.

Ultra intelligence allowed the Allies to track and neutralize German U-boats that could threaten the invasion fleet, and showed the German naval operations in the Channel, ensuring safer passage for Allied landing forces.

There was other crucial intelligence the Allies could access. It was revealed that Field Marshal Erwin Rommel, responsible for defending Normandy, would be away from his command on June 6, attending his wife's birthday, a perfect time for the Allies to strike. Rommel's absence delayed the German response to the landings.

The ability to predict German responses gave Allied commanders greater confidence in their plans, reducing uncertainties in such a complex operation. With accurate intelligence, the Allies could focus their resources where they were most needed, ensuring the invasion's success.

While D-Day was undoubtedly costly in terms of casualties, intelligence from codebreaking helped avoid catastrophic losses by ensuring the Allies avoided the most fortified areas and neutralized key German threats in advance.

The Double Cross System

The Double Cross System (or XX System) was a sophisticated British intelligence operation that turned captured German spies into double agents, by MI5, Britain's counterintelligence agency. These double agents were used to feed disinformation to the Germans, supporting Allied deception operations, particularly in the lead-up to major campaigns like D-Day. Decoded messages, including those from Enigma machines, played a critical role in making these deceptions credible.

These double agents provided false information to German handlers, carefully crafted to mislead the enemy while maintaining the agents' credibility. For example, they would mix accurate, harmless details (e.g., minor troop movements) with significant deceptions.

Decoded messages enabled the Allies to monitoring the German reaction to the false information they were being fed, and whether it was being acted upon. This feedback enabled British intelligence to refine their deceptions and ensure they were effective.

The Allies used the Double Cross System to support major deception operations, such as Operation Fortitude. Decoded messages revealed that the Germans had accepted the deception, allowing the Allies to proceed with confidence.

Battle of Midway

Breaking the Japanese JN-25 naval code, had a decisive impact on the Battle of Midway in June 1942. This pivotal intelligence breakthrough allowed the United States Navy to anticipate and counter Japan's plans.

Cryptanalysts at Station HYPO intercepted Japanese communications referring to an operation targeting "AF." Suspecting "AF" referred to Midway, U.S. cryptographers sent a false message from Midway reporting a water shortage. When Japanese communications confirmed "AF" was low on water, it verified that Midway was the target of Japan's upcoming operation.

Codebreaking revealed critical details of Japan's plan, including the timing, and objectives of their fleet, and that four aircraft carriers would be involved.

Admiral Chester W. Nimitz was therefore able to prepare an ambush. He deployed his three available aircraft carriers—USS Enterprise, USS Hornet, and USS Yorktown—near Midway well before the Japanese arrived. He also strengthened Midway's air and ground defenses, enabling coordinated attacks from both the island and carrier-based aircraft.

During the battle, the U.S. located and attacked the Japanese fleet before it could launch a coordinated strike. Within hours, U.S. aircraft sunk four Japanese carriers—Akagi, Kaga, Soryu, and Hiryu—crippling Japan's carrier strike force and causing irreparable losses in experienced pilots and crew.

The victory at Midway was a turning point in the Pacific War. It halted Japanese expansion and put them on the defensive for the remainder of the conflict. The destruction of four carriers and the loss of elite aviators significantly weakened Japan's ability to conduct offensive operations.

CHAPTER 7: THE MORAL DILEMMA IN PROTECTING THE ENIGMA SECRET

The Allies faced a significant moral dilemma regarding the use of intelligence derived from breaking the German Enigma cipher: how to exploit this vital information without revealing to the Germans that their encryption had been compromised. Maintaining the secrecy of the breakthrough, known as Ultra intelligence, often required difficult decisions where the loss of lives and destruction of assets were weighed against the long-term strategic advantage.

❖ *DID YOU KNOW*

- Ultra intelligence was the codename given to the highly valuable intelligence gathered from decrypted German military communications

- The significance of Ultra intelligence remained a closely guarded secret for many years after the war. Its true value was not widely known until the 1970s when it was revealed that much of the Allied success in World War II had been aided by this crucial intelligence.

If the Allies acted on every piece of decrypted intelligence, the Germans might notice a pattern, suspect their codes had been compromised, and change their encryption methods or machines. The result could be a catastrophic loss of intelligence capabilities, undoing years of effort by cryptanalysts.

Acting too frequently or overtly on Ultra intelligence could yield immediate tactical victories but jeopardize the long-term advantage. The Allies had to selectively decide when and how to act on intelligence to maintain the Germans' confidence in Enigma's security.

Examples of Deliberate Inaction

Convoy Attacks

Decoded messages often revealed the locations of German U-boats hunting Allied convoys. However, rerouting every convoy or deploying forces too effectively risked tipping off the Germans. The British adopted strategies like dispatching air patrols to areas where U-boats were already suspected, making the actions appear coincidental rather than informed by decrypted intelligence.

Bombing Raids

Intelligence from Enigma could pinpoint valuable targets, such as German military factories or troop movements. However, if the Allies repeatedly bombed locations identified through Ultra, it might have raised suspicions.

The Battle of the Atlantic

Protecting merchant convoys carrying vital supplies to Britain was a top priority, but acting too decisively against U-boats risked revealing the source of intelligence.

The Allies used a tactic called the "Chaff Method", where reconnaissance planes were sent on wide sweeps to "stumble upon" U-boats, masking the fact that their locations had been determined through codebreaking.

German Troop Movements in Greece (1941)

When Ultra revealed German plans to reinforce their position in Greece, the British debated whether to intervene. It was decided not to interfere with troop movements to avoid exposing their ability to read Enigma-encoded messages. The Germans remained unaware of the breach, but it allowed their reinforcements to arrive and solidify control over Greece.

The Battle of Crete (1941)

Ultra revealed German plans to invade Crete using airborne troops, but the British did not act decisively enough. There was hesitation from the British, concerned that acting too overtly might tip off the Germans that their Enigma messages were being read. The Germans successfully invaded Crete, though at a high cost, and they did not suspect their communications had been compromised.

North African Campaign (1942)

During the North African campaign, Ultra provided vital intelligence about German and Italian supply lines, troop movements, and plans.

The Allies avoided targeting every convoy or supply depot identified through Ultra intelligence. Instead, they conducted carefully timed attacks and used other sources, such as air reconnaissance, to "confirm" targets.

For example, in the Battle of El Alamein, Ultra intelligence played a key role in Allied success, but precautions were taken to ensure that the Germans attributed their losses to conventional tactics rather than codebreaking.

Ethical Considerations

Decisions not to act on Ultra intelligence often meant allowing attacks or losses that could have been prevented. Leaders bore the heavy moral burden of knowing they were deliberately withholding life-saving information, to save others.

Protecting the secrecy of codebreaking ensured the Allies could continue using Ultra intelligence to win the broader war, potentially saving millions of lives in the long term.

Civilians, sailors, and soldiers were often the ones who paid the price for the strategic decision to withhold action. This created ethical questions about whose lives were deemed expendable.

CHAPTER 8: A CRUCIAL CONTRIBUTION TO THE WAR EFFORT

The efforts of the World War II codebreakers were nothing short of extraordinary, and their contributions to the Allied victory cannot be overstated. Their ability to crack the sophisticated codes of the Axis powers—whether it was the Enigma machine, the Lorenz cipher, or the Japanese Purple code—provided critical intelligence that shaped the course of the war. Through their tireless work, the Allies gained insights into enemy plans, troop movements, and strategies, often staying one step ahead in ways that were crucial to key victories.

The secrecy of their work, and the monumental sacrifices they made, meant that their role in the war remained hidden for decades. However, the truth is clear: their breakthroughs shortened the war and saved countless lives. By deciphering enemy communications, they were able to foil numerous attacks, disrupt supply lines, and give Allied forces a strategic advantage at critical moments. The Battle of the Atlantic, the D-Day invasion, and even the Pacific theatre, were all influenced by their invaluable contributions.

In the end, the work of these codebreakers helped to turn the tide of the war and diminish the Axis powers' ability to maintain coordination and secrecy. Their legacy extends far beyond the war itself, laying the foundations for modern cryptography, intelligence, and the technologies that shape the world today.

Without their efforts, the war would have likely lasted longer, and many more lives would have been lost. The unsung heroes of World War II's codebreaking efforts stand as a testament to the power of intelligence, innovation, and unwavering dedication in the face of immense challenges.

SPIES

CHAPTER 1: UNSUNG HEROES OF THE SHADOW WAR

World War II was not only fought on battlefields but also in the clandestine world of espionage, where bravery, cunning, and resourcefulness could determine the fate of nations. Spies became some of the war's most vital yet unsung heroes, operating in the shadows to gather critical intelligence, sabotage enemy operations, and sow misinformation. Their efforts often shaped the course of key battles, saved countless lives, and contributed to the ultimate Allied victory. These individuals came from all walks of life—military officers, civilians, resistance fighters, and even double agents—united by their shared determination to undermine the Axis powers.

Who Were the Spies of WWII?

The world of WWII espionage was as diverse as the war itself. Spies included members of organized intelligence agencies like Britain's Special Operations Executive (SOE), the American Office of Strategic Services (OSS), and Germany's Abwehr, as well as ordinary citizens recruited to work behind enemy lines. Women played a significant role, with figures like Virginia Hall, an American with a wooden leg, serving as a key SOE operative in France, and Noor Inayat Khan, a British-Indian wireless operator who courageously transmitted intelligence until her capture and execution. Resistance fighters in occupied countries also acted as spies, using their local knowledge to disrupt German operations.

The Axis powers had their share of spies as well, including German operatives who infiltrated Allied territory and Japan's intelligence network in Asia. However, the Allies often held the upper hand in intelligence, thanks to extensive networks, groundbreaking codebreaking efforts, and the daring work of individuals who risked everything for the cause.

Why Were Spies Important?

Spies were critical to the war effort because they provided information that traditional military and diplomatic channels could not access. They gathered intelligence on enemy troop movements, supply chains, and fortifications, which allowed Allied commanders to make informed decisions. For example, intelligence from resistance networks in France was essential to the planning and success of D-Day, as it identified German defensive positions along the Normandy coast.

In addition to gathering intelligence, spies engaged in sabotage operations to disrupt the Axis war machine. The destruction of railways, bridges, and supply depots by Allied operatives delayed German reinforcements and supplies at critical moments. Spies also played a key role in deception operations, such as Operation Fortitude, which convinced the Germans that the D-Day invasion would occur at Pas de Calais rather than Normandy, ensuring the element of surprise.

The Risks They Took

The life of a WWII spy was fraught with danger. Operatives faced the constant threat of betrayal, capture, torture, and execution. In occupied territories, even being suspected of aiding the Allies could lead to death. Wireless operators, whose transmissions were essential for relaying information, were particularly vulnerable, as their signals could be traced by the enemy. Many spies, including brave individuals like Noor Inayat Khan and Dutch resistance fighter Hannie Schaft, paid the ultimate price for their service.

The risks extended to their families and communities, who often suffered reprisals if an operative's activities were discovered. Yet, despite the peril, these men and women persevered, driven by a sense of duty, patriotism, or the desire to resist oppression.

What They Achieved

The contributions of WWII spies were far-reaching and profound. Their intelligence shortened the war and saved countless lives by enabling precision in military planning. Codebreakers and spies working together ensured success in pivotal battles, such as the Battle of Midway, to defeat a superior Japanese fleet.

Sabotage missions delayed Axis advances, while deception campaigns diverted resources. British spies and double agents played a crucial role in ensuring the success of D-Day, the Allied invasion of Normandy on June 6, 1944. Double agents like Juan Pujol García, known as Garbo, fed false information to the Germans, convincing them to allocate forces to Calais rather than the actual invasion site at Normand. Their contributions were part of a broader deception strategy designed to mislead Nazi Germany about the true location of the invasion, making the Germans divert their forces away from the real landing site.

The bravery of these operatives often turned the tide in favor of the Allies.

Why They Did It

Motivations for becoming a spy were as varied as the individuals themselves. Some were driven by patriotism or a deep hatred of the Axis regimes and their atrocities. Others sought to protect their countries, families, and way of life. Many in occupied territories joined the fight out of a desire to resist oppression and reclaim their freedom.

For some, espionage was an extension of their skills or careers, such as diplomats, military officers, or linguists recruited for intelligence work. For others, it was a matter of personal conviction. Despite their differing backgrounds and motivations, these spies shared a willingness to risk everything for the greater good.

Challenges of Wartime Spying: Risks, Betrayal, and Constant Threat

Spying during World War II was one of the most dangerous and mentally taxing roles in the conflict. Operatives worked in a shadowy world of secrecy and subterfuge, where every action carried enormous risk. The challenges they faced were as much about surviving day-to-day threats as they were about achieving their missions. Betrayal, capture, and the relentless pursuit by enemy intelligence services created a constant atmosphere of danger.

The Risks of Betrayal

Spies operating in enemy-controlled areas often relied on local contacts for shelter, transport, and information, but these contacts were not always trustworthy. Double agents or informants, motivated by money, coercion, or ideology, frequently betrayed them to the enemy. Resistance movements and spy networks were especially vulnerable to infiltration, where a single betrayal could expose an entire cell, leading to arrests and executions. Additionally, the lack of secure communication posed significant risks. Wireless transmissions, vital for coordination, were susceptible to interception and tracing, and any compromise of codes or encryption methods could unravel entire operations.

The Threat of Capture

Spies in occupied territories operated under constant surveillance, navigating environments filled with military police, informants, and checkpoints. Their survival often depended on forged documents, disguises, and fake identities to evade capture. Those who were caught faced brutal interrogation and torture aimed at extracting information about their missions and networks.

Operatives like Noor Inayat Khan endured horrific treatment, often sacrificing their lives to protect critical secrets. Captured spies were considered illegal combatants rather than prisoners of war, leading to swift execution without trial. Methods of execution included firing squads, hangings, and public displays designed to intimidate local populations.

Operating Under Constant Threat

Spies faced immense challenges in maintaining their cover, often adopting new identities and backstories. A single mistake, such as an unfamiliar accent, a misstep in local customs, or a minor inconsistency in forged documents, could lead to exposure. To avoid detection, wireless operators frequently relocated, but their average survival time in enemy territory was alarmingly short—often just six weeks!

Living undercover also meant enduring constant paranoia, as trust was a rare commodity. Spies lived in fear of betrayal by friends, allies, or even family members, leading to a heavy psychological toll from months or years of isolation. Adding to these difficulties were resource constraints, including unreliable communication equipment, insufficient training, and limited funding, requiring operatives to rely on improvisation and quick thinking to succeed.

CHAPTER 2: THE SPY ORGANIZATIONS

Britain's Special Operations Executive (SOE)

The Special Operations Executive (SOE) was Britain's wartime organization tasked with conducting covert operations, and espionage behind enemy lines. Formed in July 1940 by Prime Minister Winston Churchill, the SOE became a key player in the shadowy world of espionage, sabotage, and resistance support. Churchill famously instructed the organization to "set Europe ablaze," to destabilize enemy territories by supporting resistance movements, sabotaging critical infrastructure, and gathering intelligence.

❖ *DID YOU KNOW*

- *The SOE was often called 'Churchill's secret army', and also the 'Ministry for Ungentlemanly Warfare'!*

Tasks and Activities

The SOE's responsibilities were broad and highly ambitious. Its operatives engaged in activities across Europe, Asia, and beyond:

1. Sabotage

Sabotage was a key tactic used to undermine the Axis war effort, targeting critical infrastructure such as railways, bridges, and factories. These acts disrupted supply lines and communication networks, causing logistical chaos. A notable example was the Norwegian heavy water sabotage missions of 1942–1943, which successfully hindered Germany's efforts to develop nuclear weapons.

2. Supporting Resistance Movements

SOE agents played a vital role in supporting resistance movements across occupied territories by providing training, equipment, and coordination. In France, the SOE worked closely with the French Resistance, carrying out operations to disrupt German forces and infrastructure, particularly in the lead-up to D-Day, significantly aiding the Allied invasion efforts.

3. *Espionage*

Agents were deployed to infiltrate enemy lines and gather crucial intelligence on troop movements, industrial production, and fortifications. They also established wireless communication networks to transmit this information to Allied command, ensuring timely and effective strategic decisions.

4. *Propaganda*

Spreading anti-Axis propaganda was vital in undermining enemy morale and fostering resistance. Through radio broadcasts and leaflet drops, operatives influenced public opinion in occupied territories, encouraging defiance against Axis forces and bolstering support for the Allied cause.

5. *Assistance to Allied Military Campaigns*

Resistance groups and operatives played a crucial role in supporting Allied landings in North Africa, Italy, and France by sabotaging enemy reinforcements and assisting local resistance fighters. They also collaborated with organizations like the Special Air Service (SAS) and the Office of Strategic Services (OSS) to coordinate efforts and maximize the impact of their operations.

❖ *DID YOU KNOW*

- *On May 5, 1941 Georges Bégué, a radio operator, became the first SOE agent parachuted into German-occupied France.*

- *By 1945, SOE was a major organisation with agent networks extending across Occupied Europe and East Asia, and had over 13,000 men and women in its ranks.*

- *The SOE had a research and development unit, Station IX, where secret weapons were developed. An early form of 'Q branch' from James Bond!*

It developed the Sleeve Gun, a silenced tube containing a .32 calibre round that an agent could conceal up a shirt or jacket sleeve. When they needed to use it, the agent simply slid it into their grip and pressed a button to fire the bullet, before slipping it back up their sleeve!

Example Operations

The SOE's impact was substantial, though difficult to measure precisely due to the secretive nature of its operations. Some examples of operations include:

Operation Postmaster (1942)

The daring mission at Santa Isabel, on the island of Fernando Po (now Bioko in Equatorial Guinea), aimed to seize German and Italian ships docked in the neutral Spanish-controlled port. These ships had enough supplies and ammunition to keep Germany's U-Boat fleet operational in the Atlantic almost indefinitely, making their removal crucial for disrupting Axis maritime operations in the region. However, because the ships were in a neutral port, a direct attack risked triggering a diplomatic incident. The operation demanded precision, stealth, and secrecy to avoid intervention by Spanish authorities.

The operation was led by Gus March-Phillipps, founder of the SOE's Small Scale Raiding Force (SSRF), also known as No. 62 Commando. A team of SOE agents and commandos, including naval specialists, underwent rigorous training for the mission. They sailed from Britain in a converted trawler, Maid Honor, taking 6 weeks to reach their target. The plan involved boarding the targeted ships under cover of darkness, incapacitating their crews, and towing the vessels out of the harbor without drawing attention.

On the night of January 14–15, 1942, the SOE team executed their mission by approaching the harbor. The raiders boarded the vessels, subdued the crews with minimal resistance, and quickly cut the mooring lines. The ships were then towed out to sea by the motor launches. The operation was a complete success, with all three vessels captured without significant damage or casualties, and taking just 30 minutes in total! The ships were taken to Lagos, Nigeria, and put into service with the Allied forces.

The aftermath of the operation caused a diplomatic stir, as it violated the neutrality of Spanish territory. In response, the British government officially denied any involvement, and no significant repercussions followed. However, the removal of the vessels had a significant impact, as it disrupted Axis intelligence operations in the region.

The operation proved that covert, deniable operations (what today would be called 'Black Ops') could succeed, and encouraged Churchill and the military to expand the SOE's operations.

❖ **DID YOU KNOW**

- *Ian Fleming, the creator of James Bond, worked in the SOE. It's thought that Gus March-Phillipps, and his actions were the inspiration for James Bond.*

Major Gus March-Phillipps

Operation Jedburgh (1944)

This was a crucial operation in support of D-Day. daring and unconventional mission where Allied teams were parachuted into France to aid and organize the French Resistance. These teams, known as "Jeds," played a pivotal role in the success of the Allied invasion by sowing chaos behind enemy lines, in France, Belgium and the Netherlands.

Resistance groups, guided by the Jeds, destroyed railway lines, derailed trains, and ambushed German convoys.

The sabotage efforts organized by the Jeds and the Resistance created chaos for the German military. Train derailments, roadblocks, and destroyed bridges forced German units to divert resources to repair infrastructure, slowing their response to the Allied invasion. By the time German reinforcements arrived at the Normandy beaches, the Allies had already established a strong foothold.

Jedburghs in front of B-24 just before night takeoff

Operation Harling (1942)

The objective of Operation Harling was to disrupt Axis supply lines by destroying the Gorgopotamos railway bridge in German-occupied Greece. The bridge was a critical link on the route supplying Rommel's forces in North Africa.

A team of SOE operatives parachuted into Greece and coordinated with the Greek resistance, including both the ELAS and EDES factions, despite their ideological differences.

On the night of November 25-26, 1942, the combined forces launched a surprise assault on the heavily guarded bridge. They successfully destroyed the structure with explosives, halting German rail traffic for weeks, demonstrating the effectiveness of sabotage in undermining Axis logistics.

Operation Foxley (1944)

While this operation didn't proceed, it showed the thinking and daring of members of the SOE. This was a plan to assassinate Adolf Hitler in an attempt to swiftly end the war, either via poison or a sniper attack. The plan was to assassinate Hitler during his morning exercise at Berghof, his country residence, while he walked alone and unprotected. A sniper was recruited and briefed, and the plan was submitted, but it had considerable opposition among British authorities and was never carried out.

Challenges and Controversies

Despite its successes, the SOE faced several challenges. Many agents were captured, tortured, and executed by the Gestapo and other Axis forces, which highlighted the high risks involved in their operations. Security breaches also occurred, with networks being compromised due to betrayals or the actions of double agents. Additionally, coordination with resistance groups was not always smooth, as ideological and logistical differences sometimes created friction, complicating efforts to work together effectively.

Legacy

The SOE left an indelible mark on the history of unconventional warfare. It pioneered methods of guerrilla warfare and sabotage, influencing the development of post-war special forces such as the SAS. Operatives like Virginia Hall, Noor Inayat Khan, and Violette Szabo became icons of bravery and sacrifice, embodying the risks and dedication of covert missions. The SOE's efforts played a pivotal role in Allied victories in key regions, demonstrating the effectiveness of covert operations in modern warfare and shaping the future of special forces.

The SOE exemplified Churchill's vision of fighting a total war, using every available means to undermine the Axis powers. Its daring missions, although fraught with danger, contributed significantly to the Allied war effort

The Office of Strategic Services (OSS): America's First Spy Agency

The Office of Strategic Services (OSS) was the United States' wartime intelligence agency during World War II and the precursor to the modern Central Intelligence Agency (CIA). Formed in 1942 under the leadership of William J. Donovan, the OSS played a critical role in espionage, sabotage, and the coordination of resistance movements. Despite its relatively brief existence, the OSS laid the foundation for post-war intelligence and special operations.

William Joseph ('Wild Bill') Donovan, Head of the OSS

Before the OSS, the U.S. had no centralized intelligence organization, relying instead on fragmented efforts from the State Department, military branches, and the FBI. Recognizing the need for a cohesive intelligence agency, President Franklin D. Roosevelt authorized its creation in June 1942.

The OSS was tasked with gathering and analyzing intelligence, conducting sabotage and psychological warfare, and supporting resistance groups in Axis-occupied territories.

Tasks and Activities

The OSS undertook a wide range of operations across multiple theaters of the war:

1. Intelligence Gathering

OSS agents infiltrated enemy territories to gather crucial intelligence on troop movements, industrial production, and military strategies. These operatives included military personnel, civilians, and foreign nationals who were sympathetic to the Allied cause, providing vital information that contributed to key Allied military operations.

2. *Sabotage and Subversion*

The OSS sabotaged Axis infrastructure, including railways, bridges, and factories, to disrupt enemy operations and supply lines. It developed a range of ingenious weapons and tools, such as time-delay explosives, silenced pistols, and concealed devices, allowing operatives to carry out covert attacks with minimal risk of detection.

3. *Support for Resistance Movements*

The OSS collaborated closely with resistance groups across Europe and Asia, providing them with weapons, training, and strategic guidance to strengthen their efforts against the Axis powers. It supported the French and assisted guerrilla operations in Burma, where local fighters played a crucial role in disrupting Japanese control.

4. *Psychological Warfare*

The OSS employed propaganda to undermine enemy morale and spread disinformation. Radio broadcasts, leaflets, and false intelligence were used to confuse and mislead enemy soldiers, disrupt their communication, and create distrust among their ranks.

5. *Special Operations*

Specialized units, such as Operational Groups (OGs) and Jedburgh Teams, conducted guerrilla warfare and coordinated with local resistance fighters.

6. *Research and Analysis*

The OSS employed scholars and experts to analyze intercepted data, providing valuable insights to military planners.

The OSS intelligence efforts were crucial in shaping strategies for major campaigns, including the Normandy invasion (D-Day) and the Italian campaign, as well as disrupting Japanese supply lines and weakening their control over the region. Additionally, OSS personnel played a vital role in gathering intelligence about Germany's V-1 and V-2 rocket programs, providing the Allies with critical information that could be used to counter these weapons.

Before Operation Torch, the Allied invasion of North Africa in late 1942, a dozen OSS officers traveled to the region, establishing local networks and gathering intelligence that was vital to the successful Allied landings. Prior to D-Day, paratroopers in the Special Operations (SO) branch of the OSS parachuted into Nazi-occupied France, Belgium and the Netherlands to coordinate air drops of supplies, meet up with local resistance forces and make guerrilla attacks on German troops

It OSS pioneered many modern intelligence techniques and tools that would influence future operations. It developed advanced encryption devices, utilized aerial photography for reconnaissance, and employed psychological warfare methods to destabilize enemy forces.

The OSS had its issues – sometimes a lack of coordination with military commands, some operations suffering from insufficient training or poor planning, and security breaches, from captured or betrayed operatives, jeopardized some of its missions, revealing the risks inherent in clandestine work. However, left behind a powerful legacy. It trained a generation of intelligence professionals, many of whom would later serve in the CIA after its formation in 1947. Its emphasis on unconventional warfare and covert operations significantly influenced the development of post-war special forces, and modern intelligence operations.

Notable Figures

• *Virginia Hall:* An OSS operative and former SOE agent, Hall was one of the most effective Allied spies in occupied France, organizing resistance networks and coordinating sabotage.

- ***Moe Berg:*** A former professional baseball player turned OSS agent, Berg collected intelligence on Germany's nuclear program.

- ***Detachment 101:*** This OSS unit in Burma worked with local Kachin tribes to wage guerrilla warfare against Japanese forces, achieving significant successes.

❖ DID YOU KNOW

- *At its peak in 1944, nearly 13,000 people worked for the OSS, with 7,500 deployed overseas. Identities remained classified until 2008.*

- *The OSS had an Emergency Sea Rescue Equipment Section. It developed a shark repellent to coat explosives used against German U-boats. Sharks were known to set off the underwater explosives by bumping into them!*

The Soviet Union's NKVD

The NKVD (Narodnyy Komissariat Vnutrennikh Del), or People's Commissariat for Internal Affairs) was the Soviet Union's primary state security and intelligence agency during World War II. Known for its ruthlessness, the NKVD played a dual role in internal security and external espionage, including the infiltration of German ranks. Its operations were pivotal to the Soviet war effort, contributing to the USSR's survival and eventual victory against the Axis powers.

Tasks and Responsibilities

The NKVD was tasked with a wide range of internal and external functions, including:

1. Counterintelligence (SMERSH)

SMERSH (Smert' Shpionam, or "Death to Spies") was a division of the NKVD created in 1943 to counter Nazi infiltration and espionage. Its role included detecting and eliminating German spies and saboteurs. It also worked to maintain Soviet discipline, targeting potential dissent within the Red Army.

2. Infiltration of German Ranks

It actively placed agents within German military and intelligence structures, as well as within Axis-allied governments. Operatives often posed as defectors, civilians, or collaborators to gain access to sensitive German plans. Fake communication operations were used to feed false information to German intelligence and disrupt their operations.

3. Espionage in Occupied Territories

It organized resistance cells in Nazi-occupied Eastern Europe, supplying them with intelligence, arms, and support to harass German forces. These networks also served as intelligence-gathering units, reporting on German troop movements and logistics.

4. Support for Soviet Partisans

It coordinated with Soviet partisan groups operating behind German lines. It provided training, supplies, and strategic guidance, ensuring their efforts aligned with broader Soviet military objectives.

5. Interrogation and Exploitation of German POWs

The NKVD interrogated captured German soldiers and officers, extracting valuable intelligence on troop movements, strategies, and morale. It also used captured personnel to infiltrate German networks, turning them into double agents when possible.

The NKVD achieved significant successes, but its methods were brutal and often indiscriminate, including mass executions and purges, which alienated many within the Soviet Union and occupied territories, sometimes hindering their operations.

However, through successful infiltration, the NKVD disrupted German intelligence efforts and misled the Wehrmacht about Soviet capabilities and intentions.

This played a role in the surprise of Operation Bagration, the massive Soviet offensive in 1944.

SMERSH and other NKVD units identified and neutralized numerous German agents operating within Soviet territory. Its support of with partisans significantly hampered German supply lines and contributed to the overstretching of Axis forces on the Eastern Front.

The paranoia it instilled in German ranks led to operational inefficiencies and a loss of trust within the Wehrmacht, and helping the Red Army. It also ensured Soviet dominance in the post-war Eastern Bloc.

German Spy Agencies: Abwehr and Gestapo

During World War II, Germany operated several intelligence and security agencies, each with distinct roles and areas of responsibility. Among the most prominent were the Abwehr, Germany's military intelligence agency, and the Gestapo, the secret police. While they were both involved in intelligence-related activities, their focus, structure, and effectiveness differed significantly.

The Abwehr: Germany's Military Intelligence Agency

The Abwehr was established in 1920, initially as a small unit tasked with intelligence and counterintelligence for the German military, in compliance with the Treaty of Versailles restrictions. It became a fully-fledged agency under the leadership of Admiral Wilhelm Canaris in 1935, as Germany prepared for rearmament and expansion under Adolf Hitler.

Tasks and Responsibilities

The Abwehr was responsible for both offensive and defensive intelligence operations, including:

1. Espionage

- Deploying spies to gather intelligence on Allied military capabilities, industrial production, and political strategies.

- Operatives were sent to Allied and neutral countries, often posing as civilians or diplomats.

2. Counterintelligence

- Identifying and neutralizing enemy spies and saboteurs operating in German-occupied territories.

- Collaborating with the Gestapo and SS on counterintelligence efforts, though tensions often arose between these organizations.

3. Sabotage and Subversion

- Conducting sabotage operations in enemy countries, including attacks on infrastructure and supply lines.

- Supporting fifth-column activities to undermine Allied morale and cohesion.

4. Collaboration with Resistance Groups

- Despite its role in serving the Nazi regime, the Abwehr, under Canaris, secretly supported some anti-Nazi resistance efforts, such as the July 20 Plot to assassinate Hitler.

The Abwehr achieved some early successes, such as infiltrating Allied networks and obtaining information on British military strategies. However, many of its operatives were poorly trained or betrayed by double agents, such as those working for the British Double Cross System.

Admiral Canaris, an anti-Nazi sympathizer, often hindered the Abwehr's efforts. He deliberately withheld intelligence from the Nazi leadership and occasionally leaked information to the Allies.

By 1944, growing distrust from Hitler and SS leader Heinrich Himmler led to the dissolution of the Abwehr. Its functions were absorbed into the RSHA (Reich Security Main Office) under the SS.

The Gestapo: The Secret State Police

The Gestapo (Geheime Staatspolizei) was established in 1933 by Hermann Göring as the Nazi regime's secret police, tasked with suppressing dissent and maintaining internal security. In 1934, the Gestapo came under the control of Heinrich Himmler, head of the SS, and became part of the RSHA in 1939.

Adolf Hitler and Hermann Göring in 1938

Tasks and Responsibilities

The Gestapo was not primarily a spy agency in the traditional sense but did engage in intelligence-related activities. Its main tasks included:

1. Internal Security and Surveillance

- Monitoring and suppressing political opposition, resistance movements, and any groups considered a threat to Nazi rule.

Using informants, wiretapping, and other surveillance methods to gather intelligence on suspected dissidents.

2. *Counterintelligence*

- Collaborating with the Abwehr and SD (Sicherheitsdienst, the SS intelligence agency) to identify and eliminate Allied spies and resistance networks in occupied territories.

3. *Interrogation and Repression*

- The Gestapo was notorious for its brutal methods of interrogation, often extracting confessions through torture.

- It targeted Jews, communists, resistance fighters, and other groups persecuted by the Nazi regime.

4. *Support for the Final Solution*

- The Gestapo played a key role in identifying and deporting Jews and other groups to concentration and extermination camps.

The Gestapo's effectiveness was bolstered by the widespread fear it instilled, leading many civilians to act as informants. However, contrary to its fearsome reputation, the Gestapo was not omnipresent. It relied heavily on civilian denunciations and lacked the manpower to monitor everyone.

Legacy

Both the Abwehr and Gestapo illustrate different facets of Nazi Germany's intelligence and security apparatus. While the Abwehr's espionage efforts were hindered by internal sabotage and Allied counterintelligence, the Gestapo's brutal methods ensured compliance through fear rather than effective intelligence gathering.

Japan's Spy Agencies: The Kempeitai and Tokumu Kikan

Japan operated several intelligence and security organizations during World War II, most notably the Kempeitai and Tokumu Kikan. While these agencies played significant roles in Japan's war strategy, their effectiveness was often limited by systemic issues, including poor coordination, over-reliance on brute force, and cultural misunderstandings of their adversaries.

The Kempeitai: Japan's Military Police and Intelligence Organization

The Kempeitai (Military Police Corps) was established in 1881 as a military police force for the Imperial Japanese Army. By World War II, it had expanded its role to include intelligence, counterintelligence, and security operations. It functioned similarly to a secret police force, focusing on maintaining internal discipline, suppressing dissent, and gathering intelligence in occupied territories.

Tasks and Responsibilities

1. Counterintelligence

- The Kempeitai worked to identify and eliminate Allied spies and resistance movements within Japan and occupied territories.

- It used informants, surveillance, and interrogation to gather information.

2. Espionage

- Kempeitai agents conducted espionage in Allied countries, particularly in Southeast Asia, China, and the Pacific.

- They attempted to infiltrate colonial administrations and military installations to gather intelligence on troop movements, defenses, and supply chains.

3. Suppression of Resistance

- In occupied territories, the Kempeitai used brutal methods to suppress uprisings and resistance groups. This included mass arrests, torture, and executions.

4. Control of Civilians

- The Kempeitai monitored civilians in Japan and its empire, ensuring loyalty to the war effort and suppressing any dissent.

The Kempeitai was feared for its ruthless efficiency in maintaining order and extracting information, playing a significant role in suppressing resistance in occupied territories. However, its reliance on torture and brutality often led to unreliable intelligence, as victims would say anything to stop the abuse. The Kempeitai's actions alienated local populations in occupied territories, fueling resistance rather than quelling it.

Tokumu Kikan: Japan's Special Service Agencies

The Tokumu Kikan (Special Service Agencies) were specialized intelligence units formed by the Japanese military to conduct covert operations, espionage, and psychological warfare. These units were particularly active in China, Southeast Asia, and the Pacific Islands.

Tasks and Responsibilities

1. Espionage

- Tokumu Kikan agents infiltrated Allied-held areas to gather intelligence on military plans and infrastructure.

- They established networks of local collaborators and sympathizers to expand their reach.

2. Support for Collaborators

- The Tokumu Kikan worked closely with nationalist and independence movements in colonized regions, such as the Indian National Army (INA) led by Subhas Chandra Bose, to destabilize British control.

3. Psychological Operations

- They used propaganda to demoralize Allied forces and encourage defections among colonial troops.
- Broadcasts, leaflets, and rumors were tools of psychological warfare.

Tokumu Kikan's support for nationalist movements like the INA created challenges for the Allies, particularly in India and Burma, and its infiltration efforts occasionally provided valuable intelligence. However, many operations were undermined by poor coordination and a lack of understanding of local cultures and languages. Also Allied counterintelligence efforts, such as the British Far East Combined Bureau, often thwarted Tokumu Kikan operations.

Challenges Faced by Japanese Intelligence

1. Cultural Barriers

- Japanese operatives often struggled with language and cultural differences, which limited their effectiveness in foreign territories.

2. Over-Reliance on Coercion

- The reliance on brutality by the Kempeitai alienated occupied populations, reducing the effectiveness of intelligence gathering.

3. Lack of Coordination

- Japanese intelligence agencies operated in silos, with limited coordination between the Kempeitai, Tokumu Kikan, and other military units.

4. Allied Counterintelligence

- The Allies, particularly the U.S. and Britain, successfully intercepted Japanese communications (e.g., through MAGIC and Ultra), often staying a step ahead of Japanese intelligence efforts.

CHAPTER 3: FAMOUS SPIES AND THEIR STORIES

Let's delve into the stories of the men and women who lived and worked in the shadows, often without recognition or reward. They were ordinary people thrust into extraordinary circumstances, whose bravery and ingenuity helped secure the Allied victory.

Virginia Hall (1906–1982): The Limping Lady

One of the most remarkable and courageous spies of World War II, Virginia Hall was not your average spy. Despite her infirmity, Virginia became one of the most successful spies in Nazi-occupied France. She was known as "The Limping Lady" because of the prosthetic limb she wore following a hunting accident. She gained a position in espionage history because of her courage, wit, and tenacity, and worked for both the British Special Operations Executive (SOE) and later the American Office of Strategic Services (OSS).

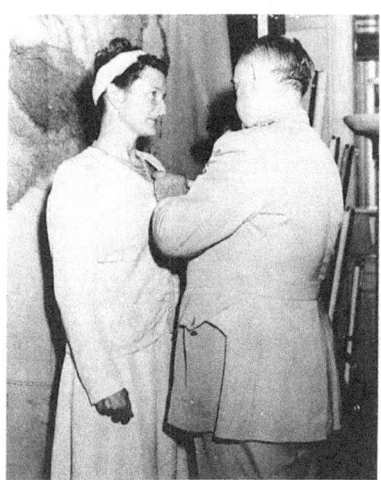

Virginia Hall receiving the Distinguished Service Cross from General Donovan

Early Life

Virginia was a driven individual who aspired to work in diplomacy, namely in the Foreign Service of the United States. Her gender and a hunting accident that left her left leg amputated below the knee, however, were the two main barriers that prevented her from achieving her goals. Virginia was not deterred in spite of this defeat. She had a fighting mentality, and her will to change the world would take her in an unexpected direction: into the field of espionage.

Joining the Special Operations Executive (SOE)

The British Special Operations Executive (SOE) recruited Virginia in 1941 when she was living in London. Virginia was motivated to prove herself in spite of her infirmity. Claiming to be an American journalist, she was transported to Vichy France, becoming the first Allied woman to be deployed behind enemy lines. Her goal was to stay incognito while gathering intelligence and provide any support she could to the local opposition.

She was unfazed by her prosthetic leg, which she lovingly called "Cuthbert." She navigated the perilous realm of Nazi-occupied France with amazing bravery and secrecy. Because of her exceptional ability to fit in with the locals, Virginia was able to establish close relationships with the French Resistance, many of whom ended up becoming her devoted supporters.

Espionage Work in France

Judging from the work she performed in France during the second world war, Virginia Hall was exceptional. Living just one step ahead of the German occupying forces and the feared Gestapo, she was a key figure in the resistance movement, intelligence gathering and assisting the safe passage of any number of Allied airmen and agents out of occupied territory. She was strong and more than that, she was very smart in organizing spies and other collaborators to dismantle Nazi military industry.

Resistance movement

An important part of Hall's work in France was her cooperation with the French resistance movement, ordinary citizens, soldiers and civilians who fought with the Nazis in a clandestine manner. These courageous persons blew up German activities, spied, and aided downed or captured allied forces to escape.

Safe Houses

Virginia personally helped set up an effective network of safe houses throughout France. These were simple dwellings, generally the house of French people who at their peril took in fugitives, agents, and other 'Resistance' people. Safe houses were essential for hiding individuals who were on the run. They offered a place for Allied soldiers, spies, and Resistance members to rest and regroup, often for extended periods. Virginia helped set up a system where people could move from one house to the next, staying hidden as they made their way towards freedom.

The people who opened their doors to these fugitives knew the risks involved. If they were caught harboring escapees, they could face execution or deportation. Yet, many French citizens willingly chose to help, demonstrating incredible bravery and dedication to the Allied cause. Virginia often relied on these unsung heroes to keep her escape routes and operations running smoothly.

Espionage: A Vast Network of Spies

Virginia Hall was not only a coordinator of escape routes; she was also a master of espionage. She built a complex network of spies to gather crucial intelligence on German troop movements, military installations, and other vital military information. Her network was as diverse as it was effective, including people from all walks of life.

Nuns and Sex Workers as Spies

Virginia recruited individuals who could access places the average spy could not. She worked with nuns who ran convents and even sex workers who "entertained" German soldiers. These women were in a unique position to gather military intelligence. Hall's network would often use these individuals to gather documents, photographs, and intelligence on German positions. The sex workers, for example, would drug their German clients and photograph their documents while they were unconscious. These were then passed on to Hall for analysis.

Unusual Tactics

The sex workers didn't just gather documents; they also helped slow down the German forces in more direct ways. Some intentionally infected German soldiers with sexually transmitted diseases. This not only incapacitated the soldiers but also disrupted the Nazis' military effectiveness by temporarily removing key personnel from the front lines. It was an unconventional tactic, but one that proved effective in the high-stakes world of espionage.

Gathering Critical Intelligence

Virginia used the intelligence she gathered to build detailed reports on German troop movements, weapon stockpiles, and fortifications. This information was sent back to London and helped the British military and Allied forces plan key operations, including the D-Day invasion. Her efforts helped give the Allies a much-needed edge in battles across France.

Escape Network: The Lifeline for Allied Airmen

Beyond her work in espionage and sabotage, Virginia Hall's most enduring legacy in France was her escape network—a lifeline for Allied airmen and agents who were shot down or captured by the Germans.

Many Allied bombers and pilots were shot down during missions over German-occupied Europe. Virginia worked with the French Resistance to ensure that these airmen could escape danger and make their way to neutral countries like Spain or Switzerland, where they could be safely returned to Allied control. She set up a system of safe houses, underground routes, and rescue operations to help them evade capture.

The escape network was not without its risks. Every successful escape meant that the network had to be even more careful and secretive. But Virginia's ability to stay one step ahead of the Gestapo and her meticulous planning made the network incredibly successful. It is estimated that she helped hundreds of men escape from German-held territories and reach safety.

The Gestapo's Pursuit

As one of the most effective and highly valued Allied spies during World War II, and as a significant threat to the German war effort, the Gestapo was desperate to capture Virginia.

The Prison Break: A Daring Rescue

The Germans laid a trap to capture Virginia and other SOE operatives. In 1942, two radio operators parachuted into France and arranged to meet other SOE operators in a safe house. Virginia was suspicious and didn't attend, but 12 SOE operatives did and were captured and jailed by the Germans who had learned of the meeting through surveillance and captured agents.

The SOE spent 6 months trying to help the operatives escape but with no success. They called on Virginia, who managed to get the prisoners moved to an outdoor camp, which she thought would make escape easier. She smuggled in escape equipment – one method was to disguise a man as a priest, put him in a wheelchair and hide a radio under his cassock! Everything went as planned and all 12 men escaped and returned to Britain! The prison break took just 12 minutes!

The Great Escape: Through the Pyrenees

Virginia's prison break effectiveness earned her the nickname "the most dangerous Allied spy" from the Gestapo, who placed her at the top of their wanted list. The Gestapo's chief in Lyon, Klaus Barbie, known as 'the Butcher of Lyon', was actively hunting her. Remaining in France would have almost certainly led to her capture, torture, and execution.

Despite constant danger, she evaded capture, even when her cover was blown. She escaped over the Pyrenees mountains into Spain—an incredible feat for someone with a wooden prosthetic leg! This trek was dangerous even for able-bodied individuals due to harsh weather, treacherous terrain, and the risk of German patrols. For Virginia, with her prosthetic leg, it was an almost insurmountable challenge.

Virginia disguised herself and joined a group of resistance members who guided her along an arduous route through the mountains, going over the highest pass as no one would imagine they'd go that way.

Despite the worst winter in 200 years with freezing temperatures, and rugged paths, Virginia refused to let her disability slow her down over the 2 day trek. At one point during the journey, she humorously reported to SOE headquarters via radio that "Cuthbert is being tiresome, but I can cope." In fact, blood was dripping down her leg from a wound. Misunderstanding her message, the SOE suggested she "get rid of him," not realizing she was referring to her leg!

Her escape over the Pyrenees is still remembered as one of the most incredible acts of personal courage in the history of espionage.

Joining the OSS

Not content with the brave work and risks she had already taken, Virginia wanted to return to France, but the British refused, saying it was too dangerous, and offered her a job in London. She refused, and in 1944, Virginia joined the OSS, the precursor to the CIA.

She returned to France, disguised as a French peasant. In fact, she went to extreme lengths to appear more realistic - she had her teeth ground down! She coordinated resistance activities in preparation for the D-Day invasion – over 500 French resistance fighters learned to fight under her command - helping to disrupt German supply lines, blowing up bridges, disrupting communications and capturing hundreds of German. President Eisenhower said the French Resistance had shortened the war by 6 months.

Post-War Life and Legacy

After the war, Virginia became one of the first women to serve in the CIA.

She rarely spoke about her wartime achievements, maintaining the secrecy she had embraced as a spy. Virginia received numerous accolades, including the Distinguished Service Cross, the only civilian woman to receive this honor during World War II. She was also made a member of the Order of the British Empire (MBE).

Virginia Hall's commitment to rescuing POWs and aiding escapees exemplified her bravery and ingenuity. Despite the immense dangers she faced, her actions had a profound impact on the war, demonstrating the extraordinary contributions of individuals working behind the scenes in occupied Europe

Noor Inayat Khan (1914–1944): A Muslim Princess Turned Wireless Operator

Noor Inayat Khan was a British-Indian spy, musician, and author who served as an SOE agent during World War II. She is remembered for her courage, resilience, and selflessness in the face of grave danger. Despite her peaceful upbringing and background, she became one of the war's most remarkable and tragic heroines.

Noor Inayat Khan

Early Life

Born in 1914 in Moscow to an Indian father and an American mother, Noor was raised in France and later moved to Britain. Her family was deeply spiritual, and Noor grew up with a commitment to nonviolence and compassion. After her family moved to France, Noor studied child psychology at the Sorbonne and became a writer, publishing children's stories and poetry.

Joining the War Effort

When World War II broke out, Noor and her family fled to England after the German occupation of France.

Noor had a unique cultural heritage, and her background made her highly adaptable and resourceful. She was well-educated and had a deep sense of service, and believed in fighting for freedom and justice which influenced her decision to join the war effort. She joined the Women's Auxiliary Air Force (WAAF) as a radio operator, where her fluency in French made her a standout candidate.

Noor was recruited by the SOE and trained as a wireless operator, one of the most dangerous roles in espionage.

SOE Mission in France

After receiving extensive training in espionage, radio operations, and covert techniques, Noor was sent to France in 1943, where she worked as a radio operator for the French Resistance, under the codename "Madeleine". Noor was part of the Prosper Network, an SOE group working with the French Resistance. Her role was to transmit messages between Resistance groups and SOE headquarters in London.

Wireless operators like Noor faced extreme danger; they could be located by German radio detection units if they transmitted for too long in one location. She successfully operated in Paris under dangerous conditions, transmitting messages to help organize sabotage and intelligence-gathering activities. Despite being constantly at risk of detection, she continued her work for several months.

The Challenges She Faced

Shortly after her arrival, the Prosper Network was betrayed, and many of its members were arrested. Despite this collapse, Noor continued to transmit vital intelligence to London, making her the only wireless operator left in the Paris area.

She frequently moved to avoid detection, often carrying her bulky radio equipment on her back and operating under intense pressure. The Gestapo tracked her movements and launched an intense manhunt for her.

Capture and Imprisonment

In October 1943, Noor was betrayed by a French collaborator and arrested by the Gestapo.

Despite being interrogated and tortured, she refused to give up any information about her mission or the Resistance. Noor was sent to Germany, where she was held in a prison and continued to resist the German authorities. She even attempted to escape twice but was recaptured each time.

Deportation and Execution

After being held in captivity for almost a year, Noor Inayat Khan was executed at Dachau concentration camp in 1944. She was 30 years old at the time of her death. Her last word was reportedly "Liberté" (Freedom) - a final declaration of her unwavering commitment to justice and the liberation of those oppressed by Nazi rule.

Legacy

Noor Inayat Khan was posthumously awarded the George Cross, one of Britain's highest civilian honors for bravery, and the Croix de Guerre by France.

She is remembered not only for her extraordinary courage but also for her gentle spirit and commitment to justice.

A memorial bust of Noor stands in London, the first memorial in Britain to an Asian woman of her kind.

Memorial of Noor Inayat Khan, London

Juan Pujol (Garbo) (1907 – 1988): The greatest double agent of WW2

Juan Pujol (1907–1988), a Spaniard who operated under the alias "Garbo", is widely regarded as one of the most brilliant double agents in history. His espionage work during World War II played a crucial role in the success of the Allied invasion of Normandy on D-Day in 1944. Pujol's ability to deceive the German intelligence services with an entirely fictitious spy network allowed the Allies to mislead Nazi forces about the timing, location, and scale of the invasion, ultimately contributing to the success of the Normandy landings.

Juan Pujol

Background and Decision to Become a Spy

In 1940, during the early stages of World War II, Pujol was living in Spain, which was neutral during the war. Motivated by a strong sense of duty and a desire to contribute to the defeat of Nazi Germany, Pujol decided that he had to do his part for "the good of humanity." He wanted to help Britain, which was at the time Germany's only adversary.

In January 1941, Pujol made several attempts to offer his services as a spy to the British Embassy in Madrid. He approached them three times, including once with the assistance of his wife (who would later be removed from his memoirs). However, his offers were rejected. The British did not take him seriously, and his repeated applications were dismissed.

Undeterred, Pujol decided to adopt a different approach. Rather than waiting for the British to accept him, he approached the Germans and offered his services as a Spanish agent. In essence, Pujol set himself up as a German spy. His goal was to gain the trust of Nazi intelligence so that, when the time was right, he could offer himself to the British as a double agent.

Creation of the "Garbo" Network

By 1942, the British finally agreed to recruit Pujol, realizing that they needed someone who could feed misinformation directly to the German intelligence services. Pujol's real strength lay in his ability to create a completely fictitious spy network, which he called his "Garbo Network." This network of fake spies allowed him to deceive the Germans into believing he had a vast network of agents across Spain, Portugal, and Vichy France.

Pujol's reports to the Germans were a mix of completely fictional information, genuine, but trivial information, and valuable military intelligence, which he intentionally delayed to give the Allies a tactical advantage. His German handlers trusted him completely – his deception was so effective that his German controllers were unaware that he was working for British intelligence.

Pujol sent over 500 radio messages between January 1944 and D-Day. At times, he would send up to twenty messages a day. His communications were so frequent and detailed that they overwhelmed the German intelligence officers. Pujol's ability to fabricate an elaborate web of false information about the location and timing of the Allied invasion played a key role in confusing and misdirecting the German military.

Operation Fortitude: A Deceptive Masterstroke

Pujol's most significant contribution came during Operation Fortitude, a massive deception operation designed to mislead the Germans about the D-Day invasion.

The goal of Operation Fortitude was to convince the Germans that the Allied invasion would take place at Pas de Calais, the narrowest point between Britain and France, rather than at Normandy, where the actual invasion occurred. By focusing the Germans' attention on a non-existent build-up of Allied troops at Calais, the Allies could land at Normandy with fewer German reinforcements and greater success.

Pujol played a central role in this deception. As part of Fortitude South, he sent multiple messages to the German intelligence services—including reports about fake troop movements and phony plans. He made the Germans believe that the Allied forces in England were preparing to cross the English Channel at Calais, with the Normandy landings serving as a distraction.

The day after D-Day, Garbo sent a message to the Germans that the Normandy landings were just a diversion, and that the main invasion force was still preparing to land at Calais. This message was passed directly to Adolf Hitler, who, believing the deception, ordered German troops in Calais to remain in place to protect against the non-existent invasion. In fact, there were more German troops in Calais two months after D-Day than there had been on D-Day itself!

The German delay in reinforcing Normandy allowed the Allied forces to establish a stronghold on the French coast. This contributed to the success of the Normandy invasion and ultimately led to the liberation of France.

Recognition and Honors

For his brilliant work, Juan Pujol received military decorations from both sides of the war!

Pujol was awarded the Iron Cross by the Germans for his work as a German agent, despite the fact that he was secretly working for the Allies!

Pujol was also honored by the British, receiving the Member of the Order of the British Empire (MBE) for his exceptional contribution to the Allied war effort.

Post-War Life and Anonymity

After the war, Pujol feared that the Nazis might seek reprisals against him for his role in the deception operation. To avoid the risk of retaliation, he worked with MI5, the British intelligence agency, to fake his own death. Pujol traveled to Angola in 1949, where he staged his death from malaria, and his wife—whom he had divorced—told their children that their father had passed away.

Pujol eventually moved to Lagunillas, Venezuela, where he lived under a new identity, running a bookstore and gift shop. He lived in relative anonymity, never revealing his true identity.

It wasn't until the 40th anniversary of D-Day, on June 6, 1984, that Pujol's true identity was revealed. He traveled to Normandy to pay his respects to the fallen soldiers, and it was only then that the world learned about the man who had played such a pivotal role in the success of the D-Day invasion.

Legacy

Juan Pujol, under his alias Garbo, remains one of the most remarkable double agents in history. His ability to manipulate and deceive the Germans, to the point where he was able to feed them complete fabrications without their ever suspecting him, is a testament to his genius as a spy. He played a pivotal role in the success of D-Day and the Allied victory in Western Europe.

Today, Pujol is remembered not only for his role in World War II espionage but also for the extraordinary lengths to which he went to protect his own identity and safeguard his family from Nazi retribution. His story is a remarkable example of how deception, intelligence, and bravery can turn the tide of war.

❖ DID YOU KNOW

- *Because the Allies had broken the Enigma codes, they knew exactly how the Germans reacted to the MI5-controlled intelligence fed by the agents like Garbo, and knew they believed every word he said!*

Violette Szabo (1921 – 1945): An Heroic SOE Agent and Symbol of Resistance

Violette Szabo was a courageous British secret agent and member of the SOE. Known for her incredible bravery, determination, and sacrifice, Violette played a critical role in organizing and supporting resistance efforts in Nazi-occupied France. She remains one of the most revered figures in the history of espionage, a symbol of resilience and sacrifice against tyranny.

Violette Szabo

Early Life

Violette Szabo was born on June 26, 1921, in Paris, France, to a British father and a French mother. Her upbringing was shaped by a blend of British and French cultures, which she embraced throughout her life. Fluent in both English and French, she spent her early years moving between England and France, experiencing the differences and challenges of both nations.

In 1940, during the early days of World War II, Violette married Étienne Szabo, a French Foreign Legion officer. Their marriage, however, was tragically short-lived. In 1942, Étienne was killed in action in North Africa. Violette, now a young widow with a baby daughter, was devastated by the loss of her husband. Yet, instead of retreating into grief, she found purpose in his memory and her determination to contribute to the war effort against the Nazi occupation.

Joining the SOE

Motivated by the death of her husband and driven by a strong desire to fight the Nazi regime, Violette made the decision to join the SOE. Violette's fluency in French and her deep understanding of French culture made her an ideal candidate for missions in Nazi-occupied France, where she was tasked with supporting the French Resistance. Violette's experience as a widow and her previous understanding of military tactics gave her the resilience and fortitude needed for the dangerous missions she would soon undertake.

Missions in France

First Mission (April 1944)

In April 1944, Violette was parachuted into Vichy France as part of an operation to assist local Resistance groups. Her role was to gather intelligence on German troop movements, disrupt German supply lines, and help lay the groundwork for the upcoming D-Day invasion. She also played a key role in organizing sabotage operations that targeted German supply lines, disrupted transportation, and hindered the Nazis' ability to move troops and materials efficiently across France. She also provided logistical support to the Maquis, the French Resistance fighters.

After completing her mission, Violette returned to England, where she debriefed her superiors and prepared for another, more dangerous mission.

Second Mission (June 1944)

After the success of D-Day in June 1944, Violette was sent back to France to assist the French Resistance in central France. Her mission was to organize sabotage operations and coordinate resistance efforts to disrupt German reinforcements coming from the east, hindering their ability to support German forces in Normandy. She worked with the Maquis to destroy supply depots, railroad tracks, and communication lines vital to the German war effort.

Despite her courage and success in these operations, Violette's mission became perilous as the Gestapo began closing in on the Resistance cells, and her cover was blown.

Capture and Imprisonment

During her second mission, Violette was captured by the Germans after a fierce gunfight near Limoges. In an attempt to help her comrades escape, she provided covering fire and fought valiantly but was ultimately captured.

Violette was taken by the Gestapo, who interrogated and tortured her for information. Despite the brutality she endured, she never revealed any details about her mission, the Resistance, or her comrades.

Even in the face of horrific treatment, Violette's determination and resilience remained unbroken. She remained loyal to the British cause, refusing to betray her comrades and fellow Resistance fighters. Her courage and defiance under torture inspired all those who heard of her bravery.

Deportation and Execution

Violette's fate was sealed when she was deported to Ravensbrück concentration camp, one of the most notorious camps for female prisoners in Nazi Germany. Conditions at the camp were horrific, and many prisoners did not survive.

In early 1945, just 23 years old, Violette Szabo was executed by the Nazis at Ravensbrück. She died a hero, but her legacy has endured, and she is remembered as one of the bravest women to serve in WWII.

It is believed that Violette's final word was "Liberté" (Freedom), symbolizing her lifelong commitment to the fight for freedom, justice, and liberation from tyranny.

Legacy

Violette Szabo's courage and selflessness have made her a lasting symbol of bravery and sacrifice. Her contributions to the Allied war effort were crucial, and her story continues to inspire generations of men and women in the fight against oppression.

She was awarded the George Cross for bravery, for her exceptional courage and sacrifice in the face of certain death. She was also awarded the Croix de Guerre by France for her bravery and service to the French Resistance.

Her story was immortalized in the 1958 film, "Carve Her Name with Pride," based on the biography written by R.J. Minney. The film depicted her extraordinary heroism and served as a testament to her unwavering dedication.

A memorial to Violette stands in Lambeth, London, near where she lived, ensuring that her legacy is never forgotten.

Violette Szabo's life and sacrifice continue to symbolize the crucial role that women played in wartime espionage and the fight against Nazi oppression.

Duško Popov (1912 – 1981): "Tricycle"

Dušan "Duško" Popov, codenamed "Tricycle," was a Serbian intelligence agent during World War II, and one of the most incredibly daring and successful double agents, working for the British while feigning allegiance to the German Abwehr. Born on July 10, 1912, in Titel, Austria-Hungary (now Serbia), Popov came from a wealthy family and was educated in law at the University of Belgrade and the University of Freiburg.

Dušan "Duško" Popov

In 1940, Popov was recruited by the German military intelligence service, the Abwehr, due to his extensive business connections across Europe. He was tasked with gathering intelligence on Britain and its military capabilities. However, Popov harbored a deep aversion to Nazism and, recognizing the threat it posed to Europe, chose to offer his services to the British. He approached MI6, the British foreign intelligence service, and proposed to act as a double agent.

The British accepted his offer, assigning him the codename "Tricycle" because he was the "big wheel" of an espionage team that included another man and a woman as the "little wheels."

Operating under this guise, Popov provided the Germans with misleading and inaccurate information, thereby feeding disinformation to the enemy. He made 14 trips to Lisbon during the war to meet face-to-face with his German handlers. He was the only one of the double agents who was allowed by MI5 to take the risk of meeting up with his controllers when he passed on intelligence material; the other agents sent their material by wireless transmitters.

One of his most significant contributions was his involvement in Operation Fortitude, the D-Day deception campaign. By conveying false intelligence, Popov played a crucial role in convincing German military planners that the invasion would occur in Calais, not Normandy, thereby facilitating the success of the D-Day landings.

Popov's lifestyle mirrored that of a James Bond character; he was known for his charm, womanizing, and high-society connections. His personal life and exploits were as daring as his espionage activities, and he is thought to be another one of the inspirations for Ian Fleming's fictional character, James Bond.

Johnny Jebsen (1917 – 1944): 'Artist'.

Jebsen's story is one of daring missions, espionage, and ultimately tragic capture by the Germans.

Johnny Jebsen

Johnny Jebsen, whose real name was Johann-Nielsen Jebsen, was born in Hamburg and had a background that made him well-suited for work in espionage. He had German ancestry and spoke fluent German, which would later serve him well during his spy activities in Nazi-occupied Europe. Jebsen was an undercover agent who was recruited by the SOE.

At the outset of World War II, Jebsen joined the German military intelligence agency, the Abwehr, largely to avoid compulsory service in the army. In 1940, Jebsen recruited Popov, whom the Germans hoped to recruit as an agent. On his recruitment, Popov immediately offered his services to the Allies as a double agent.

From 1943 onwards, Johnny Jebsen was a double agent in the service of the Allied cause, while continuing to claim to be a staunch German loyalist. Jebsen was privy to some of the most important Allied secrets: the real plans for the Normandy landings, and a major operation aimed at disorienting the Germans that the landings would take place on other sectors of the Normandy beachhead.

Jebsen's luck ran out in 1944. British intelligence learned a devastating piece of information just four weeks before the launch of D-Day - that Jebsen, was about to be arrested in Lisbon and taken to Berlin for interrogation. Jebsen had recruited Popv and also knew enough about Garbo to expose the whole Double Cross system if he broke under torture – the success of D-Day was at stake!

The Gestapo was aware of the importance of SOE operatives and worked relentlessly to break them. Jebsen's ability to resist interrogation and his refusal to betray his comrades were testament to his courage.

He was presumed executed by the Germans in 1944 as part of their brutal reprisals against spies and Resistance members. His work, however, contributed significantly to the Allied cause during the war.

Odette Sansom (1912 – 1995): "Lise"

Odette Sansom, codename 'Lise' was a French-born British secret agent and one of the most extraordinary women spies in the Second World War. Having escaped from the Germans to England, Sansom was recruited by the SOE.

Odette Sansom

Deployed to France in 1942, Odette was assigned to work with the SPINDLE network, led by SOE operative Peter Churchill. Her primary tasks included organizing resistance groups, arranging the distribution of supplies, and coordinating with local operatives to disrupt German operations. She also couriered messages, intelligence, and materials between resistance members and Allied contacts.

Odette operated under the constant threat of exposure. In 1943, the SPINDLE network was betrayed by a double agent, and she was arrested by the Gestapo, along with Peter Churchill.

Odette endured brutal torture 14 times, at the hands of the Gestapo. Her back was scorched with a red-hot poker and all of her toenails were pulled out, but she refused to disclose critical information about SOE operations or spies.

She misled her captors by claiming that Peter Churchill was her husband and a relative of Winston Churchill, hoping to protect him and elevate their perceived importance to the Germans, which might prevent execution.

Odette was eventually sent to Ravensbrück concentration camp, where she endured harsh conditions and near starvation. Despite the suffering, she remained defiant and continued to resist her captors.

❖ **DID YOU KNOW**

- *Odette was aided in her endurance in prison by the example of her grandfather, who "did not accept weakness very easily."*

Odette survived the war and was awarded several medals. Including an MBE and the George Cross (she remains the only woman to have received the George Cross while alive).

❖ **DID YOU KNOW**

- *Some spies went to great lengths for their role. For instance, James Hutchison, a British SOE agent, underwent plastic surgery to disguise his appearance and evade detection by the Germans - he had previously operated in France, and his cover had been blown by the Gestapo. He had the tops of his ears clipped, the bridge of his nose removed, his nose made smaller, and his chin was made more prominent! It must have been worth it though as he became the principle British liaison officer with the French Resistance.*

Fritz Kolbe (1900 – 1971): German Informant

Kolbe was a German diplomat who turned against the Nazi regime and became one of the most important informants for the Allies. Working in the German Foreign Office, Kolbe had access to critical Nazi intelligence and used this position to secretly provide the OSS with vital information about German troop movements, Nazi weapons, and the V-2 rocket program.

Fritz Kolbe

Kolbe's decision to spy for the Allies was motivated by his deepening disillusionment with the Nazi regime, particularly after witnessing the atrocities committed by the Nazis. He approached the Swiss Consulate and eventually contacted American diplomats in Switzerland to offer them highly sensitive documents.

Kolbe provided the OSS with a wealth of crucial intelligence, the key being intelligence on the development of the V-2 rockets. These rockets were part of Germany's advanced weapons program and posed a significant threat to the Allies. Kolbe's information helped the Allies target and destroy critical sites, delaying the Nazis' ability to use the rockets effectively.

He also provided information about German expectations of the site of the D-Day landings, the Messerschmitt Me 262 jet fighter, Japanese plans in Asia and exposed a spy working in the British embassy in Ankara. By the end of the War, Kolbe had passed over 1,600 documents to his handler in Switzerland.

He was described by the CIA as the most important spy of the war. Allen Dulles wrote: "George Wood (our code name for him) was not only our best source on Germany but undoubtedly one of the best secret agents any intelligence service has ever had.

Christine Granville (1908–1952): SOE Legend

Christine Granville, born Krystyna Skarbek, was a Polish-born British spy who became one of the most celebrated female agents of World War II. Known for her extraordinary courage, quick thinking, and resourcefulness, she earned legendary status as one of the SOE's most effective operatives. Her daring missions and ability to work behind enemy lines contributed greatly to the Allied war effort and made her a symbol of bravery and defiance.

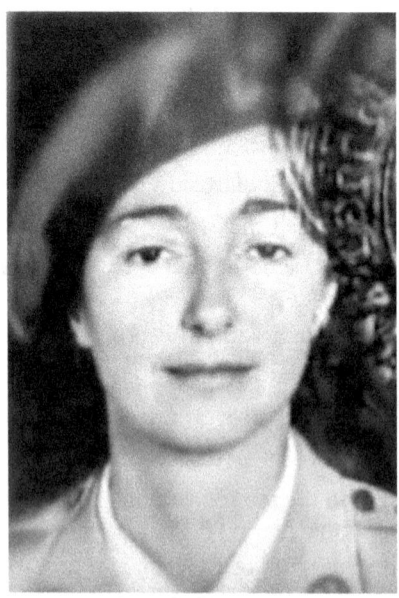

Christine Granville

❖ **DID YOU KNOW**

- *Christine Granville was the first female agent of the British to serve in the field and the longest-serving of all Britain's wartime women agents*

Born on May 1, 1908, in Warsaw, Poland, Krystyna Skarbek came from a wealthy, aristocratic family, which allowed her access to a privileged education and early exposure to the arts and languages.

Her adventurous spirit and determination were evident from a young age. Krystyna had a strong sense of patriotism and a deep love for her homeland, qualities that would drive her future actions.

When Germany invaded Poland in 1939, Krystyna's life was upended. Like many others in her position, she fled to London and joined the British war effort. It was here that her path as an intelligence agent began. She adopted the codename Christine Granville, and being fluent in Polish, French, and English, she became a key agent for the British, able to operate in some of the most dangerous areas of Europe.

Poland and Hungary: Early Espionage Work

Christine's first missions involved smuggling intelligence reports from Poland into Hungary. These missions were perilous, as she had to cross border checkpoints and evade German patrols.

One of her most audacious early feats was skiing over the Carpathian Mountains in temperatures below -40°C! The mission, which British intelligence considered a suicide mission, was particularly dangerous due to the harsh terrain and Nazi patrols. As a woman, partly Jewish, and a foreigner, she was at constant risk, but she used her quick thinking and charm to evade capture.

❖ **DID YOU KNOW**

- *During a Gestapo interrogation, Christine famously bit her tongue to fake tuberculosis symptoms, hoping to escape suspicion. Her ability to think on her feet under immense pressure was a hallmark of her bravery.*

In Bulgaria, she passed a microfilm from a Polish intelligence organisation called the "Musketeers" to the British. It contained photos of a German military buildup near the border with the Soviet Union, indicating that a German invasion of the Soviet Union was being planned. The microfilm was sent to Winston Churchill, who could scarcely believe it; but by March, with information from other sources, the Prime Minister was persuaded that Skarbek's intelligence was accurate. The Germans invaded in June 1941.

France: Organizing Resistance Networks

In 1944, Christine was parachuted into France as part of a mission to help organize and support the Maquis, in southeastern France to weaken the German occupiers prior to the Allied invasion of southern France, Operation Dragoon, which would take place on August 15, 1944.

She had to escape southern France, spending 3 weeks to walk to the Alps. Once there, she persuaded 63 Polish soldiers to mutiny against their German superiors – the German commander surrendered.

Daring Rescue of SOE Agents

One of Christine's most famous feats was her daring rescue of three SOE agents (including her commander, Francis Cammaerts) from German custody. This occurred in 1944 in the town of Digne, southern France.

With much bravado, she introduced herself as Cammaerts' wife and a niece of British General Bernard Montgomery and threatened the German in charge with terrible retribution if harm came to the prisoners. She reinforced the threat with bribery – an offer of two million francs for the men's release. The agents were released from prison!

Tragic End

After the war, Christine Granville's remarkable career as a secret agent came to an end, and she continued to live in London. In a tragic turn of events, Christine was murdered in London in 1952 by an obsessed former lover. Her sudden and violent death shocked those who knew her and left the world without one of its most brilliant wartime heroes.

Christine Granville's courage and resourcefulness is honored by a series of posthumous recognitions and memorials, including the George Medal, the Order of the British Empire (OBE) and the Croix de Guerre.

Symbol of Courage

Christine Granville became a trailblazing figure in wartime espionage and remains a symbol of courage and defiance against the Nazi regime. Her work as an agent for the SOE in some of the most dangerous and hostile areas of Europe solidified her place as a legendary figure in the fight against tyranny.

Elvira de la Fuente Chaudoir (1911 – 1996): "Bronx"

Elvira de la Fuente Chaudoir, codenamed "Bronx," was a Peruvian socialite who became a significant double agent for the British during World War II. Elvira's deceptive communications to the Abwehr are credited with preventing the 11th Panzer Division from reinforcing German forces at Normandy.

Born in 1911 to a wealthy family, Elvira led a vibrant social life across Europe, frequenting casinos and high-society events. She was persuaded to work for MI6, who then suggested she let herself be recruited by the Germans and work as a double agent.

In 1941, while in France, she was approached by Henri Chauvel, a French collaborator, and subsequently introduced to Helmut Bleil, a German spy. Bleil recruited her to gather political, financial, and industrial information about Britain for the Germans, assigning her the codename "Dorette" and arranging a monthly payment disguised as alimony. He also provided her with invisible ink for covert communications.

Upon returning to England, Elvira reported her recruitment to MI6, who then handed her over to MI5. She was incorporated into the Double-Cross System on October 28, 1942, under the codename "Bronx," inspired by her favorite cocktail. She was given a cover job at the BBC to legitimize her presence in England.

As Agent Bronx, Elvira's role involved sending letters to her German handlers containing a mix of gossip, half-truths, and deliberate misinformation. One notable contribution was her claim that Britain had stockpiled large quantities of chemical weapons, which likely deterred the Germans from initiating gas warfare.

Her most significant impact was during Operation Ironside, a plan to deceive the German army into expecting an attack in the wrong part of France. Elvira's usual form of communication was to send letters by post to Cannes, but wartime post was notoriously slow. In the case of an imminent attack, Elvira was to send a telegram to a bank based in Lisbon. Using a simple code, she wrote: 'Urgently need £50 to pay my dentist'. This translated to: 'I am certain an attack will take place in the Bay of Biscay within one week'. This was sent on May 27, 1944, 10 days before the planned invasion of Normandy on June 6. This resulted in the entire 11th Panzer being left in Bordeaux on the Bay of Biscay, awaiting an attack that would never come!

After the war, Elvira, now in her mid-30s, left the world of intelligence and retired from espionage. Instead, she opted for a quieter life back in France on the French Riviera, opening a gift shop. She died in 1996 at the age of 85.

❖ **_DID YOU KNOW_**

- *Elvira's letters to the Germans looked like any normal letter, but between each line, she used secret ink applied with a matchstick!*

Axis Spies

German espionage during World War II, led primarily by the Abwehr (Germany's military intelligence agency), the SD (Security Service of the SS), and later by the RSHA (Reich Security Main Office), played a significant role in Nazi Germany's strategy. However, while their efforts were extensive and resourceful, German espionage efforts were not as effective as those of the Allies, who often had the upper hand in counterintelligence and deception.

The Duquesne Spy Ring

The Duquesne Spy Ring was one of the largest espionage networks operating in the United States during World War II, spying for Nazi Germany. Led by Herbert John "The German Spy King" Duquesne, the ring infiltrated key industries to gather intelligence on American military installations, war production, and shipping routes. The spies used coded messages, hidden compartments, and radio transmissions to relay information to Germany.

The FBI uncovered the network in 1940 with the help of William G. Sebold, a German-American who became a double agent. Sebold's collaboration allowed the FBI to infiltrate the group, culminating in the arrest of Duquesne and 32 members in 1941. This successful operation, known as "Operation Duquesne," involved wiretaps, surveillance, and undercover agents. In 1942, the members were tried and convicted, with Duquesne receiving an 18-year sentence.

The dismantling of the ring dealt a significant blow to Nazi Germany's espionage efforts in the U.S., and demonstrated the FBI's ability to counter such threats and to serve as a warning to other potential spies.

Operation Pastorius

Operation Pastorius was a failed German espionage mission during World War II, launched in 1942 to sabotage key U.S. industrial and transportation facilities. Organized by Nazi Germany's Abwehr under Admiral Wilhelm Canaris, the operation aimed to disrupt the American war effort and spread terror. Eight agents, fluent in English and familiar with the U.S., were trained in sabotage techniques and divided into two teams. They were transported by submarines and landed on Long Island, New York, and Ponte Vedra Beach, Florida, in June 1942.

The mission quickly unraveled. On Long Island, George John Dasch, leader of the first team, aroused suspicion when burying equipment and later defected to the FBI. Providing detailed information, Dasch enabled the rapid capture of all eight operatives within weeks. Poor preparation, agent disloyalty, and effective FBI counterintelligence sealed the operation's fate.

In a military trial ordered by President Franklin D. Roosevelt, six agents were executed on August 8, 1942. Dasch and Ernest Burger, who cooperated with authorities, received reduced sentences and were deported to Germany in 1948. The failure of Operation Pastorius marked a significant blow to German espionage, exposing the weaknesses in Nazi intelligence and the difficulties of carrying out sabotage in a foreign country.

The rapid apprehension of the operatives highlighted the FBI's growing counterintelligence capabilities and led to enhanced security measures against espionage and sabotage in the United States. It was also a considerable propaganda victory for the U.S.

THE RESISTANCE

CHAPTER 1: THE RESISTANCE FIGHTERS

World War II was a conflict defined not only by massive armies and strategic battles but also by the courage and determination of resistance fighters who operated in the shadows. These brave individuals—men, women, and even teenagers—risked everything to resist Nazi and Axis occupation in Europe, Asia, and beyond. From sabotaging supply lines to gathering intelligence and aiding Allied forces, resistance fighters played an indispensable role in the fight against tyranny.

Resistance movements were as diverse as the countries they arose in. In France, the Maquisards carried out daring sabotage operations against German forces. In Poland, the Home Army (Armia Krajowa) orchestrated uprisings, most notably the Warsaw Uprising of 1944. Meanwhile, in Yugoslavia, Partisans led by Josip Broz Tito waged a relentless guerrilla war against Axis occupiers. Resistance fighters also emerged in Norway, Greece, and the Netherlands, as well as in Asian territories such as China and the Philippines, demonstrating that defiance against oppression was a universal force.

Their importance to the Allied war effort cannot be overstated. Resistance fighters disrupted Axis supply chains, derailed troop movements, and provided critical intelligence that often tipped the scales in favor of the Allies. For example, the destruction of railways and bridges delayed German reinforcements to the Normandy front after D-Day, directly aiding the success of the invasion. Resistance networks also rescued downed Allied airmen, facilitated escapes for prisoners of war, and harbored Jewish families fleeing persecution.

However, the risks they faced were staggering. Operating under constant threat of betrayal and capture, many resistance members endured torture or execution when discovered. Entire families and communities were often punished in retaliation for resistance activities. Yet, despite these dangers, countless individuals remained steadfast, driven by the hope of liberation and a vision of a free world.

The legacy of these resistance fighters is one of unparalleled bravery and sacrifice. Their stories remind us of the power of ordinary people to stand against overwhelming odds and fight for freedom and justice. Without their contributions, the outcome of World War II—and the course of history—might have been very different.

Why WWII Resistance Was Crucial

Operating in occupied territories, resistance fighters carried out daring missions that disrupted enemy operations, supplied essential intelligence, and directly supported Allied forces, using their local knowledge and expertise. Their efforts not only weakened the Axis war machine but also kept alive the hope of liberation in countries under occupation.

Sabotaging the Enemy

Resistance movements dealt significant blows to Axis infrastructure through acts of sabotage. They destroyed railways, bridges, and communication lines, which disrupted the movement of troops, supplies, and weapons. For example:

- France's Maquisards coordinated sabotage efforts to delay German reinforcements after the D-Day landings, which was critical to the Allies' success in Normandy.

- Norwegian saboteurs, such as those in the Norwegian Heavy Water Sabotage operation, attacked facilities crucial to Germany's nuclear program, halting their progress toward developing atomic weapons.

These operations forced Axis forces to divert manpower and resources to repair and guard infrastructure, weakening their ability to sustain their war efforts.

Gathering Intelligence

Resistance fighters were instrumental in gathering intelligence that proved crucial to Allied planning. They observed enemy troop movements, identified strategic targets, and passed this information to Allied command via clandestine communications networks.

For example, members of the Polish Resistance provided early reports of Nazi atrocities and detailed plans of the German V-2 rocket program, allowing the Allies to target launch sites effectively. Dutch resistance networks that warned of German troop deployments, assisting Allied operations in Western Europe.

This intelligence often provided the Allies with a critical edge, enabling them to anticipate and counter Axis strategies.

Supporting Allied Forces

Resistance fighters actively supported Allied operations by providing safe havens, assisting in escape efforts, and engaging enemy forces directly.

In Italy, partisan groups harassed German units and supported the advancing Allied armies during the Italian Campaign. In France, military units such as the Special Air Service (SAS) and Special Operations Executive (SOE) parachuted in troops and agents who coordinated with local resistance fighters, supplying weapons and training to bolster their effectiveness. Resistance groups also rescued and sheltered downed Allied airmen and prisoners of war, ensuring their safe return to combat or freedom.

Inspiring Hope and Defiance

Beyond their tactical contributions, resistance movements had a profound psychological impact. They kept the spirit of defiance alive in occupied territories, rallying civilians to resist the occupiers and refusing to let Axis powers feel secure in their control. The very existence of these movements symbolized the resilience of occupied nations and galvanized Allied support for liberation efforts.

Occupation: Life Under Axis Control and the Courage to Resist

Life under Axis occupation during World War II was marked by fear, oppression, and brutality. For millions across Europe, Asia, and beyond, the daily reality involved strict controls, economic exploitation, and the ever-present threat of violence. Yet, even in the face of overwhelming adversity, ordinary people risked everything to resist, motivated by a sense of justice, freedom, and the hope of a better future.

The Axis powers imposed harsh regimes over occupied territories, tailoring their actions to align with strategic and ideological goals. Under Nazi occupation, the regime enforced its ideology of racial superiority through the systematic persecution and extermination of Jews, Slavs, Roma, and other targeted groups. Ordinary citizens endured mass executions, deportations, forced labor, and severe restrictions on freedom. Similarly, Japanese occupation in East and Southeast Asia was marked by terror and exploitation, including the mass killing of civilians, forced labor, and infamous atrocities such as the Nanjing Massacre and the use of "comfort women."

Occupied territories were exploited economically, stripped of resources to sustain the Axis war efforts. In Europe, German authorities requisitioned food, goods, and industrial output, often leaving local populations impoverished and facing famine. In Asia, Japanese forces seized farmland and labor, causing widespread starvation and suffering among local communities.

They also tried to erase local culture, and identities and replace them with their ideologies. Schools, media, and religious institutions were co-opted to spread propaganda, while any form of dissent was ruthlessly crushed. This atmosphere of repression was reinforced by fear and control mechanisms, including spy networks, collaborators, and secret police forces such as the Gestapo in Europe and the Kenpeitai in Asia. These organizations created an ever present sense of danger, where betrayal could lead to torture or death, leaving citizens in constant fear of speaking or acting against the occupiers.

Why Ordinary People Resisted

Despite the immense risks, countless civilians chose to resist Axis occupation, driven by diverse motivations rooted in their personal experiences and values. For many, resistance was an expression of patriotism—a determination to defend their homeland's sovereignty and preserve its culture against foreign domination. Others were fueled by moral outrage at the brutal treatment of civilians, mass executions, and persecution of minorities, unable to remain passive in the face of such atrocities. The hope that their actions could hasten the end of Axis control inspired many to act, even at great personal cost.

Personal loss also played a powerful role, as those who had suffered tragedies—such as the loss of loved ones to occupation forces—sought revenge or justice. Additionally, Allied propaganda and underground networks encouraged resistance, offering solidarity and hope. Radio broadcasts like the BBC's French Service served as a rallying cry, urging citizens to stand up against oppression and join the fight for liberation. These shared motivations unified individuals from diverse backgrounds in their courageous stand against tyranny.

The Risks of Resistance

Resistance fighters faced unimaginable dangers as they stood against Axis occupation. Betrayal was a constant threat, with informants and collaborators capable of exposing entire resistance networks, often resulting in arrests, brutal torture, and executions.

The consequences of their actions extended beyond individual fighters, as Axis forces frequently carried out harsh reprisals, punishing entire communities for resistance activities. Mass executions, the destruction of villages, and other collective punishments were grim realities.

For instance, one of the worst Nazi atrocities on the Nazi-occupied Island of Crete, occurred on December 13, 1943. In retaliation for Greek resistance activities, the Nazis entered the town of Kalavryta where they then separated older boys and men from the women and children. The 438 men and boys were taken to a field and executed. 13 men survived, only because they were hidden under the bodies of the dead. The women and children were locked in primary school, which the Germans then set on fire. Luckily, the women and children found a way to escape the school.

After the Drama uprising in Greece in 1941, Bulgarian forces killed 3,000 people in Drama alone, and an estimated 15,000 Greeks in the weeks following the uprising.

The Viannos massacre on Crete in September 1943, saw the execution of over 500 Cretans, along with burning and looting of villages. The German Commander responsible for ordering the massacre, Friedrich-Wilhelm Müller, was executed after the war.

❖ **DID YOU KNOW**

- *When the SAS attacked German airfields on Crete, they left behind British flags and other clues to their identity, in the hope that the local population would not be blamed for the attacks.*

Operating in secrecy added to the strain, as resistance members were often unable to trust even close friends or family. This isolation left them vulnerable, both emotionally and physically, as they navigated a perilous path in their fight against tyranny.

Acts of Defiance

Despite the immense challenges, resistance fighters found innovative and courageous ways to strike back against Axis forces. They sabotaged railroads, factories, and supply lines to disrupt military operations and weaken the occupiers' infrastructure. Underground newspapers were distributed to counter Axis propaganda, spreading information and bolstering morale among oppressed populations.

Many resistance members risked their lives to hide fugitives, including Jews, Allied airmen, and escaped prisoners of war, providing them shelter and safe passage. Some also carried out targeted assassinations of collaborators and high-ranking

Axis officials, directly challenging the enemy's control and striking symbolic blows against the occupation.

CHAPTER 2: RESISTANCE MOVEMENTS OF WORLD WAR II

The French Resistance

Many of the 'Maquis', French resistance guerilla fighters, had joined the resistance to avoid being forced into the 'Service du travail obligatoire' (STO) – Compulsory Work Service – which supplied forced labour for the Nazis. Hundreds of thousands of French men and women had been shipped eastwards to work in the German's arms factories and other key industries.

The French Resistance worked closely with the British SAS - for instance, the Autun raid in 1994 involved the SAS and the French Resistance, led by Pierr La Roche. The Germans were desperately running short of fuel for its tanks and planes, and the objective of the raid was to make this situation worse, by destroying the German fuel depot at Autun. The plant was destroyed, burning for 4 days! Producing 7,500 gallons of fuel a day, the plant's destruction had a significant effect on the German war effort.

❖ ***DID YOU KNOW***

- *The French Resistance had an estimated 50,000 members. More than 90,000 were killed, tortured or deported by the Germans.*

- *Marcel Pinte probably was the youngest French resistance fighter – he was just 6 years old! Marcel hid secret messages under his clothes and delivered them behind enemy lines to resistance leaders.*

French Resistance members during the battle of Paris in August 1944

As part of Operation Dingson, the Resistance worked with the French SAS to destroy German lines of communication, set ambushes and undertake sabotage to hinder the convoys of German reinforcements circulating in Brittany and heading towards Normandy after D-Day. The operation showed the effectiveness of joint operations in undermining German military capabilities in occupied France.

The intelligence networks were by far the most numerous and substantial of Resistance activities, passing on information of military value such as details of the coastal fortifications of the Atlantic Wall or German deployments in France. By 1944, the BCRA (the French intelligence service) was receiving 1,000 telegrams by radio every day and 2,000 plans every week. Many radio operators, called pianistes, were located by German goniometers. Their dangerous work gave them an average life expectancy of just six months!

The French Resistance was especially key in assisting the Allies after the invasion of Normandy on D-Day in 1944. Three-man special forces 'Jedburgh' teams made up of British, American and French personnel in uniform were dropped into France to align French resistance activities with Allied strategy. They also helped to undermine German defences in Normandy by disabling rail, communication and power networks in the invasion area. This disruption helped prevent the Germans from concentrating their strength in Normandy on D-Day and in the weeks that followed.

The Vercors Uprising was a significant resistance effort by the French Maquis (members of the French Resistance) during July 1944 in the Vercors plateau region of southeastern France. The Allies encouraged the uprising, to disrupt German troop movements and communications, to help the Allied advance after D-Day. By the end of July 1944, the uprising had been crushed. Hundreds of Maquisards and civilians were killed, and the Vercors plateau was left devastated, but it had required the diversion of 10,000 German troops to deal with them.

Eisenhower said: "*Without their great assistance, the liberation of France and the defeat of the enemy in Western Europe would have consumed a much longer time and meant greater losses to ourselves.*"

As one American officer noted: "*the Resistance was so effective that it took half a dozen real live German divisions to contend with it, divisions which might otherwise have been on our backs in the Bocage.*"

❖ DID YOU KNOW

- Around 9,000 Allied pilots escaped POW camps thanks to the Franco-Belgian resistance.

- In June and July 1944, the Resistance derailed 180 trains behind the Normandy front-lines, limiting the German's ability to move troops and supplies.

- Vichy France created a paramilitary group, called the Milice, to work alongside the Germans in combating the Resistance. They were brutal, torturing and executing many Resistance fighters. After the war, France executed many of the 25,000 – 35,000 Milice for their collaboration with

Germany.

German Reprisals

The war in Europe had become brutal, and the local villagers in Franch were made to pay a heavy price by a vengeful enemy.

The massacre at Oradour-sur-Glane, on June 10, 1944, was one of the most horrific atrocities committed by the SS. 643 civilians, including men, women, and children, were massacred as collective punishment for Resistance activity in the area. The men were taken into barns where they were shot in the legs and doused with gasoline before the barns were set on fire. The women and children were herded into a church that was set on fire; those who tried to escape through the windows were machine gunned. They even murdered people who just happened to be passing the village at the time. After the massacre, the SS looted and burned Oradour-sur-Glane, leaving it in ruins.

The attack highlighted the dangers faced by the Resistance and the civilians who supported them. These reprisals were intended to discourage further resistance activities.

❖ **DID YOU KNOW**

- *President Charles de Gaulle ordered that the ruins of the old village be maintained as a permanent memorial and museum.*

Other villages suffered a similar fate. The village of Montsauche was razed to the ground by the Germans, who had ordered all villagers to leave, before shooting any that refused, and then setting the village ablaze. In Dun-les-Places, the Germans rounded up all men and executed them in the village square, and the commanders then ordered their bodies to be mutilated. The village priest was hanged from the church tower!

The Polish Underground (Armia Krajowa)

The Polish Underground State and its military wing, the Armia Krajowa (AK) ("Home Army"), were among the most significant resistance movements in Europe during World War II. The AK played a critical role in resisting Nazi occupation through sabotage, intelligence-gathering, and armed uprisings, including the Warsaw Uprising of 1944 and efforts to smuggle intelligence out of Auschwitz.

The Warsaw Uprising (August-October 1944)

The Warsaw Uprising stands as one of the most heroic yet tragic chapters in the resistance efforts of the AK. By mid-1944, as the Red Army advanced toward Warsaw from the east, the AK launched its efforts to liberate the city from German occupation before Soviet forces arrived. The uprising was driven by a desire to demonstrate Poland's sovereignty and prevent a Soviet-backed communist regime from taking control after the war.

Warsaw Ghetto uprising

On August 1, 1944, approximately 40,000 AK fighters initiated a citywide uprising, armed with a limited arsenal of small arms, grenades, and improvised weapons. They quickly captured large parts of Warsaw, but German forces responded with overwhelming firepower, including tanks, artillery, and air raids. The AK faced immense challenges, including a lack of Allied support due to logistical difficulties and political tensions with the Soviet Union. Compounding their plight was the inaction of the nearby Red Army, which halted its advance and provided no assistance, leaving the AK to fight alone.

For 63 days, the AK fought heroically against German forces, but the uprising ultimately ended in surrender on October 2, 1944. The toll was devastating, with approximately 16,000 AK fighters and 200,000 civilians killed, and the Germans systematically destroyed much of Warsaw. Despite its tragic outcome, the Warsaw Uprising remains a powerful symbol of courage and sacrifice, a cornerstone of Polish history, and a testament to the resilience of those who fought for their nation's freedom.

❖ *DID YOU KNOW*

- *By allowing the Germans to suppress the Warsaw Uprising, and the forces supporting the Polish government-in-exile in London, the Soviets faced little opposition in establishing communist control of Poland.*

Smuggling Intelligence Out of Auschwitz

The AK played a crucial role in exposing the atrocities of Auschwitz and other Nazi crimes to the world. Through a network of covert operations, the AK gathered intelligence on German activities, including those within Auschwitz. Brave prisoners, such as Polish officer Witold Pilecki, infiltrated the camp by allowing themselves to be captured. Pilecki organized resistance within Auschwitz and gathered detailed intelligence on the systematic extermination occurring there.

Smuggling information out of Auschwitz was perilous, with prisoners hiding reports in clothing, shoes, or food supplies. Trusted couriers and escapees relayed this intelligence to AK contacts outside the camp, who then transmitted it to the Polish government-in-exile and Allied forces. The intelligence, including Pilecki's detailed accounts, revealed the horrifying scale of the Holocaust and the Nazis' systematic extermination of Jews and other groups. Despite these efforts, the international response was tragically limited.

Auschwitz

The legacy of the AK is one of unparalleled courage and an unwavering commitment to Polish independence. Their efforts not only resisted occupation but also shone a light on some of the darkest chapters of human history.

❖ DID YOU KNOW

- *Of the 6 million Jews murdered by the Nazis, 1.1 million were killed at Auschwitz.*

- *Among those who tried to escape, just 196 were successful.*

The Greek Resistance

The Greek Resistance was one of the most significant and active resistance movements in occupied Europe. It emerged following the Axis occupation of Greece in 1941, with various groups organizing to oppose the German, Italian, and Bulgarian forces that had divided and controlled the country. The resistance played a critical role in sabotaging Axis operations, aiding Allied intelligence, and inspiring hope among the Greek population. By 1943, there was between 20,000 – 30,000 Greek resistance fighters!

Greek Resistance members, 2nd Division of ELAS

Resistance fighters carried out daring acts of sabotage against Axis infrastructure. For instance, in November 1942, a combined operation by the National Liberation Front (EAM) and National Republican Greek League (EDES), supported by British SOE agents, successfully destroyed the Gorgopotamos railway bridge (known as Operation Harling). This was one of the first major sabotage acts in Axis-occupied Europe, and the beginning of a permanent British involvement with the Greek Resistance. This act disrupted German supply lines to North Africa.

The Greek Resistance played a critical role in the British SOE's attacks on German airbases in Crete, at Heraklion, Maleme, and Kastelli. Resistance fighters scouted German airbases, monitoring troop movements, patrol routines, and identifying weak points in security. They relayed this information to SOE operatives, ensuring the success of sabotage efforts. Resistance members acted as guides, leading SOE agents through Crete's rugged terrain to their targets, providing safehouses and hiding spots for operatives before and after missions, and also were directly involved in carrying out the attacks.

Armed resistance groups, particularly the ELAS (Greek People's Liberation Army) and EDES (National Republican Greek League), waged guerrilla warfare in mountainous regions. These groups ambushed Axis patrols, attacked supply convoys, and liberated small towns and villages.

Resistance groups maintained clandestine communication networks to coordinate operations and spread anti-Axis propaganda. They organized escape routes for POWs and Allied personnel, helping many to flee occupied Greece.

Greeks engaged in acts of nonviolent resistance, such as strikes, protests, and the refusal to comply with Axis requisitions of food and resources. The Athens Polytechnic uprising in 1943 demonstrated the Greek people's defiance against Axis rule.

While the Greek Resistance was effective, it was also marked by internal rivalries, particularly between ELAS (led by the communist EAM) and EDES (a republican nationalist group). These factions often clashed, undermining their collective efforts against the Axis. The tensions eventually led to a civil war in Greece after the Axis retreat in 1944.

❖ **DID YOU KNOW**

- *Greece resisted the Axis forces for 219 days, more than triple the time of any other country that would come to be occupied during the war.*

- *In reference to the bravery of the Greek people, Churchill is quoted as saying, "Hence, we will not say that Greeks fight like heroes, but that heroes fight like Greeks."*

- *During the Axis occupation of the country from 1941–1944, nearly 100,000 people died of starvation.*

The Danish Resistance

The Danish Resistance's efforts to save Jewish citizens during World War II stand as one of the most remarkable and successful acts of collective bravery and humanity. The operation to ferry nearly all of Denmark's Jewish population to safety in neutral Sweden was a powerful example of resistance against Nazi oppression.

In April 1940, Denmark was occupied by Nazi Germany, but its strategic importance and diplomatic efforts allowed the Danish government to retain a degree of autonomy. For a time, Denmark's Jewish population, approximately 7,000 people, was relatively safe as the Nazis refrained from harshly enforcing anti-Jewish laws. However, this changed in August 1943 when the Danish government resigned in protest against escalating German demands, prompting the imposition of martial law. Soon after, the Nazi leadership moved to deport Denmark's Jews to concentration camps.

The rescue operation began with a crucial warning on September 28, 1943, from Georg Ferdinand Duckwitz, a German diplomat sympathetic to the Danish cause. Duckwitz leaked Nazi plans for the deportation of Danish Jews to Danish politicians and resistance leaders, providing the resistance and the Jewish community with an opportunity to act. The Danish Resistance, alongside ordinary citizens, swiftly organized efforts to hide Jewish families and ferry them to safety in neutral Sweden. Synagogues, homes, hospitals, and schools became hiding places, while fishermen and boat owners used their vessels to transport Jews across the Øresund Strait, often under the cover of night to evade German patrols.

The journey across the strait, only a few miles wide, was perilous, but the operation received broad support from Danish society. Doctors, clergy, teachers, and even police officers contributed by sheltering Jews and facilitating their escape, while financial contributions from citizens helped cover transportation costs. Over several weeks, this coordinated effort successfully saved approximately 7,200 Danish Jews and 700 non-Jewish family members by transporting them to Sweden. Only about 475 Jews were captured by the Nazis and sent to the Theresienstadt ghetto, but many survived due to continued Danish advocacy on their behalf.

The rescue of Denmark's Jews remains one of the most remarkable and successful acts of resistance and humanitarianism during World War II.

❖ DID YOU KNOW

- *The Danish resistance movement was honored as part of the "Righteous Among the Nations" at Yad Vashem (the Holocaust Remembrance Center) in Israel.*

- *"Righteous Among the Nations" refers to non-Jewish individuals who risked their lives to save Jews during the Holocaust, to honor their courageous acts of humanitarianism during a time of extreme persecution; essentially, they were "righteous" people who stood up to help others despite great danger.*

Yugoslav Partisans

The Yugoslav Partisans, led by Josip Broz Tito, were among the most successful and effective resistance movements in Europe, inflicting significant casualties on Axis forces, tying down hundreds of thousands of German, Italian, and collaborationist troops.

Formed in 1941 following the Axis invasion and occupation of Yugoslavia, the Partisans were organized under Tito, a skilled leader of the Communist Party of Yugoslavia. He united various ethnic groups under the Partisan banner and promoted a political vision to liberate Yugoslavia and establish a socialist, multi-ethnic federal state.

The Partisan campaign was characterized by classic guerrilla warfare tactics, including ambushes, sabotage, and hit-and-run attacks, which targeted Axis supply lines, railroads, bridges, and communications infrastructure, significantly disrupting enemy operations. They established liberated zones in rural and mountainous areas, creating provisional governments, schools, and hospitals, which helped consolidate their power and recruit fighters. Their movement drew broad popular support, uniting fighters from diverse ethnic and religious backgrounds—Serbs, Croats, Slovenes, Bosnians, Montenegrins, and Macedonians—despite the ethnic divisions intensified by Axis occupation and collaborationist regimes like the Ustaše in Croatia.

Initially, the Allies supported the Chetniks, a royalist resistance group, but their effectiveness waned due to frequent collaboration with Axis forces against the Partisans. By 1943, the Allies shifted their support to the Partisans, recognizing their military success and commitment to the anti-Axis cause. The Partisans engaged in significant battles such as the Battle of Sutjeska and the Battle of Neretva in 1943.

The Battle of Neretva was part of the German-led Operation Weiss (Fall Weiss), also known as the Fourth Enemy Offensive, which aimed to destroy the Partisan movement in the Balkans. The Axis forces included German, Italian, Croatian, and Bulgarian troops, totaling over 90,000 men, who launched a coordinated offensive against the Partisans in Bosnia and Herzegovina. The Partisans, numbering about 20,000, were accompanied by thousands of wounded fighters and civilians, making their situation particularly precarious. The Germans were ordered to shoot any Partisans captured, and deport hostile civilians to transit camps. Villages were to be razed to the ground.

While the Partisans did not decisively defeat the Germans or their Axis allies in direct combat during the Battle of the Neretva, they achieved their strategic objective: avoiding annihilation. By successfully escaping encirclement, they preserved their fighting force, evacuated their wounded, and maintained their ability to continue the resistance.

These battles demonstrated their resilience and strategic adaptability. By late 1944, with Soviet Red Army support, the Partisans liberated much of Yugoslavia, including Belgrade in October, emerging as the dominant military and political force in the country.

Yugoslav Partisans were instrumental in rescuing Allied pilots during World War II. One of the most notable instances of their efforts is the Operation Halyard. By 1944, Allied bombing missions over German-occupied territories, particularly targeting oil fields in Romania and key infrastructure in the Balkans, resulted in numerous aircraft being shot down. Many airmen parachuted into Yugoslavia, often landing in areas controlled by the Yugoslav Partisans, who organized their evacuation. Makeshift airstrips were constructed, enabling Allied aircraft to land and evacuate around 500, mostly American, airmen to safety.

Rescue of Allied airmen by Yugoslav Partisans

Tito's leadership was central to the Partisans' success. His charisma and strategic vision inspired loyalty and unity among his diverse forces. He promoted a federal socialist Yugoslavia that appealed to many disillusioned by nationalist ideologies, while his military acumen ensured the Partisans' survival and ultimate victory. After the war, Tito became the leader of Socialist Yugoslavia, shaping its post-war identity as a multi-ethnic federation until his death in 1980.

Czech Resistance

Following the German annexation of Czechoslovakia in 1939, the resistance grew in strength despite harsh reprisals by the occupiers.

As the war progressed, the resistance developed from isolated groups to a more organized group, under the leadership of the Czechoslovak government-in-exile based in London.

Resistance groups carried out acts of sabotage, including derailing trains, damaging industrial production facilities, and hindering German military operations. Factories producing goods for the Nazi war effort became prime targets for disruption.

Czech resistance fighters also collected intelligence on German troop movements, fortifications, and plans, often relaying this information to the Allies via clandestine radio transmissions.

Resistance members spread anti-Nazi propaganda, organized strikes, and maintained the morale of the Czech population through underground publications. These efforts aimed to foster unity and hope among the oppressed population.

The Czech Resistance undertook some notable operations including Operation Anthropoid in 1942, which saw the assassination of Reinhard Heydrich, often referred to as 'The Butcher of Prague' and 'The Architect of the Holocaust', who was the Nazi Reich Protector of Bohemia and Moravia. For the exiled Czechoslovak government in London, assassinating Heydrich was not just a military objective - it was a way to assert their relevance, inspire resistance, and demonstrate to their citizens that Nazi oppression could be resisted.

Josef Gabčík and Jan Kubiš, two young resistance fighters, were selected for the mission, and trained by the British SOE. Heydrich was killed by an anti-tank grenade, dealing a significant blow to the Nazi leadership.

Heydrich's car after the attack

In retaliation, the Nazis unleashed brutal reprisals, including the destruction of the villages of Lidice and Ležáky and the execution of thousands of Czechs. Despite the risks, Operation Anthropoid inspired resistance movements across occupied Europe by showing that even high-ranking Nazis could be targeted successfully. The bravery of Gabčík and Kubiš became legendary.

In the final days of the war, the Czech resistance spearheaded the Prague Uprising in May 1945. Civilians and fighters clashed with German forces in an effort to liberate the city before the arrival of the Red Army. While the uprising did not fully succeed on its own, it significantly weakened German control in the region.

Defending the radio station, Prague Uprising

The Chinese Resistance

The Chinese resistance during the Second Sino-Japanese War (1937–1945) was a vast and multifaceted effort against Japanese occupation, blending military campaigns with civilian-led movements. Unlike the clandestine, urban-focused French Resistance, Chinese resistance involved large-scale guerrilla warfare and conventional battles led by the Nationalists under Chiang Kai-shek and the Communists under Mao Zedong. Communist forces, such as the Eighth Route Army, excelled in hit-and-run tactics, sabotage, and disrupting Japanese control in rural areas, with civilian militias playing a critical role by providing shelter, food, and intelligence.

In urban areas, civilians resisted by sabotaging Japanese efforts, spreading propaganda, and aiding military units. Despite an early alliance between the Nationalists and Communists, internal divisions eventually resurfaced, complicating the resistance. Japanese forces responded with brutal tactics, including mass executions, village destruction, and biological warfare, making resistance perilous.

Ultimately, Chinese resistance tied down hundreds of thousands of Japanese troops, preventing their deployment elsewhere in the Pacific Theater. It was one of the largest resistance efforts of World War II, combining military action and civilian defiance on a massive scale.

Filipino Guerrillas

The Filipino guerrillas were instrumental in resisting Japanese occupation and supporting U.S. military efforts to liberate the Philippines from 1942 to 1945. Comprising former soldiers, civilians, and local leaders, guerrilla groups such as the Hunters ROTC, Hukbalahap, and forces led by commanders like Ferdinand Marcos waged a coordinated grassroots resistance. These groups employed ambushes, sabotage, and raids to disrupt Japanese operations, destroy supply lines, and gather intelligence.

Guerrillas collaborated with U.S. forces, particularly during the return of General Douglas MacArthur's troops in 1944–1945, providing vital intelligence, guiding American forces, and assisting in battles such as the Battle of Leyte Gulf and the liberation of Luzon. They also played a crucial role in rescuing Allied prisoners and harassing retreating Japanese forces.

Supported by local populations for supplies, shelter, and information, the guerrilla resistance became a widespread national effort that significantly contributed to the liberation of the Philippines.

CHAPTER 3: HEROES OF THE RESISTANCE

Resistance groups were composed of courageous men and women who risked their lives to fight Nazi occupation. These heroes came from diverse backgrounds—students, intellectuals, soldiers, and ordinary citizens. Let's take a look at some of these incredible people, and their contributions.

Jean Moulin (1899–1943)

Jean Moulin was one of the most famous and heroic figures in the French Resistance during World War II. He played a critical role in uniting various Resistance groups against the German occupation of France and became a symbol of French defiance and resilience. Moulin's efforts in organizing the Resistance in France were vital to the success of the Allied campaign and the eventual liberation of France.

Initially, Moulin worked as a secret courier between different French Resistance groups, gathering intelligence and passing on messages. He helped form connections between various Resistance factions, who at that time were often fragmented and working independently.

In 1942, he was appointed by Charles de Gaulle, leader of the Free French Forces, to unite the diverse Resistance groups into a single, coordinated movement known as the National Council of the Resistance (CNR). It was a significant achievement to unite Communists, Gaullists, and Socialists, under one collective goal! This unity was vital for organizing larger sabotage efforts, intelligence gathering, and preparing for post-liberation France.

Moulin helped coordinate the Resistance's role in preparing for the D-Day invasion and other Allied operations in France. The work of Resistance groups under his leadership included acts of sabotage, providing intelligence, and assisting downed Allied airmen and soldiers.

In June 1943, Jean Moulin was betrayed and captured by the Gestapo in the French city of Lyon. Despite being tortured for days, Moulin never revealed any information about his comrades or the Resistance network. His courage under torture made him a martyr for the Resistance movement. Moulin was eventually transported to Germany, where he died on July 8, 1943, likely from injuries sustained during his brutal interrogation.

After his death, he was posthumously promoted to the rank of General by General Charles de Gaulle. He is honored in France with many streets, schools, and monuments named in his memory. The Musée Jean Moulin in Paris is dedicated to his life and work.

❖ DID YOU KNOW

- *In 1940, Moulin refused to sign a document accusing French troops of massacring civilians (they had been killed by German bombing). Beaten and imprisoned because he refused to comply, Moulin attempted suicide by cutting his own throat with a piece of broken glass. This act left him with a scar he would often hide with a scarf.*

Nancy Wake (1912–2011)

Nancy Wake was one of the most decorated Allied secret agents of World War II. A New Zealand-born, Australian-raised journalist, she became a legendary figure for her work with the Special Operations Executive (SOE) and the French Resistance, demonstrating exceptional courage, resourcefulness, and leadership.

Nancy Wake

In her early twenties, she moved to Europe and became a journalist, witnessing the rise of Nazism in Germany and its oppressive policies. This fueled her determination to fight against fascism. She was living in France when the war broke out, where she joined the Resistance.

She worked as a courier, smuggling documents, supplies, and downed Allied airmen to safety. Her charm, quick thinking, and ability to bluff German soldiers made her highly effective. She showed incredible bravery, one cycling over 300 miles through German-occupied territory to deliver vital messages after her radio operator's equipment was damaged.

Wake's daring activities earned her the nickname "The White Mouse" because she was so adept at eluding capture. Her effectiveness drew the attention of the Gestapo, who placed her on their most-wanted list, offering a significant reward for her capture. Despite this, she continued her work undeterred.

She escaped France in 1943 via the Pyrenees and into Spain. She then traveled to Britain, and joined the Special Operations Executive (SOE), where she was trained in espionage, sabotage, and guerrilla warfare. She was parachuted back into France in 1944 to organize and support Resistance groups ahead of the D-Day invasion.

Wake became a leader among the Maquis, a group of French Resistance fighters, coordinating sabotage missions, disrupting German supply lines, and leading attacks on German troops. She engaged directly in combat, famously killing a German soldier with her bare hands during an ambush.

At one point, she led over 7,000 Maquis fighters, proving her exceptional leadership and strategic skills, and a huge achievement for a woman in those times!

Wake was highly decorated for her wartime service, receiving awards from multiple countries, including the George Medal (UK), Medal of Freedom (U.S.), Chevalier de la Légion d'Honneur and Croix de Guerre, Medaille de la Résistance (France).

After the war, she briefly entered politics in Australia and later moved to London, where she lived until her death in 2011 at the age of 98.

❖ DID YOU KNOW

- *As a freelance journalist and war correspondent, she interviewed Adolf Hitler in 1933 and attended the mass rallies. That interview changed her life and at that early stage she had decided to oppose Nazism having witnessed them beating Jews in Germany.*

Lucie Aubrac

Lucie was a member of the French Resistance and co-founder of the Libération-Sud movement. She organized sabotage missions, attacking the railway stations at Cannes and Perpignan. She also distributed over 10,000 anti-Nazi flyers.

In 1943, she orchestrated a daring operation to rescue her husband, Raymond Aubrac, and other Resistance leaders from Gestapo custody. She visited Klaus Barbie, the notorious Gestapo 'Butcher of Lyon'. She was told Raymond would be executed but she could marry him first (she had pretended they were only engaged). When Raymond was being brought back to prison after "wedding", he and fifteen other prisoners were rescued by a commando unit led by Lucie, who attacked the vehicle he was in, killing the six guards

In 1996, Lucie was awarded the Legion of Honor by the French government for her heroism during World War II.

Andrée De Jongh (1916–2007)

Andrée De Jongh was a remarkable Belgian resistance fighter and the founder of the Comet Line, one of the most successful escape networks during World War II. Her bravery and ingenuity helped hundreds of Allied airmen evade capture and safely return to Britain, making her a legendary figure in the history of the Resistance.

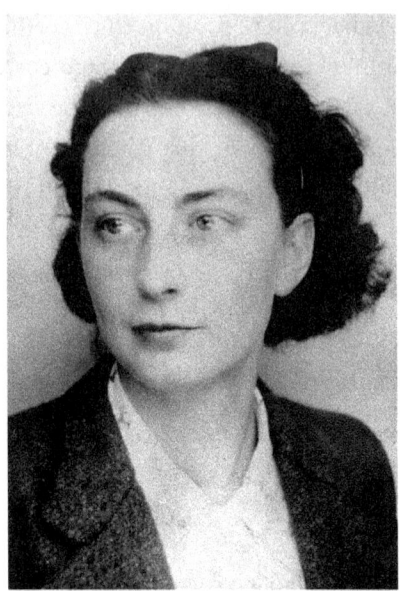

Andrée De Jongh

Inspired by the stories of wartime heroism during World War I and driven by her hatred for the Nazi regime, she decided to actively resist after Belgium was occupied in May 1940.

In 1941, at just 24 years old, Andrée founded the Comet Line (or "Le Réseau Comète") to assist Allied airmen shot down over occupied Europe. This was an escape route which stretched from Belgium through France to the Pyrenees Mountains, where the escapees would cross into neutral Spain and eventually make their way to Gibraltar, and then Britain. Andrée herself often guided escapees, escorting them by train and on foot through dangerous Nazi-occupied territory. She personally escorted over 100 airmen across the Pyrenees, a journey that required immense physical stamina and nerves of steel.

Her father, Frédéric, also became deeply involved in the network. Tragically, he was arrested by the Nazis in 1943 and executed at the KZ Buchenwald concentration camp.

In January 1943, Andrée was betrayed and arrested by the Gestapo in Urrugne, near the Spanish border, while leading a group of escapees. Despite intense interrogation and torture, she refused to reveal information about the Comet Line or her collaborators.

She was deported to Ravensbrück and Mauthausen concentration camps, enduring harsh conditions but surviving until the war ended in 1945.

After the war, Andrée was celebrated as a heroine of the Resistance. She was awarded numerous honors, including, The George Medal (UK), The Medal of Freedom with Bronze Palm (USA), and the Croix de Guerre (Belgium and France).

Despite her fame, she remained humble, emphasizing the collective efforts of the Resistance.

The Comet Line had a significant impact on the Allied war efforts, successfully guiding approximately 800 Allied airmen to safety. The courage of Andrée and her team of couriers, safe house operators, and guides played a vital role in supporting the Allied war effort.

After the war, Andrée worked as a nurse in leprosy hospitals in Africa, continuing her commitment to service and humanity.

She passed away on October 13, 2007, at the age of 90, leaving behind a legacy of extraordinary bravery and selflessness.

❖ DID YOU KNOW

- *Andrée asked the British to pay the Comet Line's expenses, but the British were sceptical that a young woman was capable of smuggling airman out of Nazi-occupied Europe over a distance of 500 miles. They initially thought she was a German spy! They eventually agree to her request.*

- Andrée's codenames were Dédée and Cyclone, reflecting her bravery, temperament and unbridled energy.

Georges Guingouin (1913 – 2005)

Guingouin, French Communist Party member, was the leader of the Maquis in the Limousin region. He commanded guerrilla forces that disrupted German supply lines and staged ambushes against occupying troops. In 1943, his unit destroyed the Busy-Varache viaduct, and then sabotaged a rubber factory near Limoges, halting the production five months. They also sabotaged the subterrain cable between the Bordeaux submarine base and Berlin. He was also involved in the Battle of Month Gargan, one of the rare occasions when the Resistance fought the Germans in open battle – the Marquis lost 97 men, while the Germans lost 342, despite being heavily outnumbered.

His group liberated towns, including Limoges without a shot being fired. Guingouin, greeted as a hero, was rewarded by being elected mayor of Limoges in 1945.

Henri Rol-Tanguy (1908 – 2002)

Rol-Tanguy was a Communist Resistance leader and head of the French Forces of the Interior (FFI) in Paris. When Allied armies approached Paris in August 1944, Rol-Tanguy's forces took part in the liberation of Paris. After five days of fighting,

German General Dietrich von Choltitz notified Colonel Rol that he was ready to negotiate. Alongside Free French General Philippe Leclerc de Hauteclocque, Tanguy accepted and signed the act of surrender on August 25, 1944.

Joseph Epstein (also known as Colonel Gilles 1911 – 1944)

Epstein was a Jewish Polish immigrant and French Resistance leader. He joined the French Foreign Legion in 1939, but was captured and imprisoned by the Germans. He escaped to Switzerland, was deported to Germany where he escaped again, this time to Paris!

He then joined the Francs-Tireurs et Partisans (FTP) communist resistance group in Paris.

He led a small group of 12 men, who attacked a formation of German soldiers in Paris. Dozens of soldiers were killed and only one resistance fighter. The Germans reported that they'd been attacked by hundreds of resistance fighters!

Epstein was captured, tortured and executed by the Nazis in 1944, along with 19 other FTP members.

Sophie Scholl (Germany 1921 – 1943)

Scholl was a member of the White Rose group, a nonviolent anti-Nazi resistance movement at the University of Munich in Germany. The group was a powerful example of youthful resistance to the Nazis.

The group was known for distributing thousands of anti-Nazi leaflets across Germany, highlighting Nazi war crimes, calling for resistance, and encouraging sabotage of the German war machine.

The last pamphlet published said: "Even the most dull-witted German has had his eyes opened by the terrible bloodbath, which, in the name of the freedom and honour of the German nation, they have unleashed upon Europe".

On February 22, 1943, Scholl was executed by guillotine by the Gestapo at just 21 years old, becoming a symbol of resistance in Nazi Germany.

❖ *DID YOU KNOW*

- *The sixth leaflet was smuggled into Britain where it was reprinted and dropped over Germany by Allied planes.*

Witold Pilecki (Poland 1901 – 1948)

Pilecki was one of the founders of the Secret Polish Army, one of the first resistance groups in Poland. Astonishingly, Pilecki deliberately allowed himself to be captured and sent to the Auschwitz concentration camp to gather intelligence – at the time, little was known about the camp, and many thought it was just an internment camp.

Witold Pilecki

While in Auschwitz, Pilcecki organised the Military Organization Unit, with the aim of improving moral among the inmates, to provides news from outside, to distribute extra clothing and food, to setup intelligence networks and to prepare inmates to take over the camp in the event of a relief attack. By 1942, his network was using a homemade radio to deliver messages on the number of arrivals and deaths in the camp.

His reports on the atrocities at Auschwitz were vital in alerting the world to the horrors occurring there. Pilecki hoped that either the Allies would drop arms or troops into the camp, or that the Home Army would organize an assault on it from outside, which didn't materialize. On April 27, 1943, Pilecki successfully escaped from Auschwitz!

During the Warsaw Uprising, Pilecki commanded a company of troops, but was captured by the Germans and imprisoned as a POW, where he remained until liberation in 1945.

❖ **DID YOU KNOW**

- *In 1947, he was arrested by the Polish communist authorities on charges of working for "foreign imperialism" and, after being subjected to torture and a show trial, was executed in 1948.*

Le Chambon-sur-Lignon (France)

This time, we're looking at a village rather than a specific person! Le Chambon-sur-Lignon is a small French village known for its resistance to the Nazis, led by its Protestant pastor, André Trocmé, and the community.

Between December 1940 and September 1944, the inhabitants of the village sheltered over 3,000 Jewish people (and 2,000 others fleeing Vichy France), saving them from deportation to concentration camps. They forged ID and ration cards, and in some cases, guided them to neutral Switzerland.

These actions were very unusual in involving the whole population, with no-one informing the Germans. Much of the population were descendants of Huguenot (Calvinist) Protestants, who were persecuted by the Catholic authorities in previous centuries, so they understood the suffering of a minority.

Whenever the villagers got wind of impending visits by the Vichy police or German Security Police raids, they moved the refugees further into the countryside. In 1943, the Germans raided a school and arrested 5 students who they said were Jewish. They were sent to Auschwitz where they died. They also arrested the teacher, who the SS executed.

❖ **_DID YOU KNOW_**

- *In 1990, Israel recognized all the inhabitants of Le Chambon and those of nearby villages collectively as "Righteous Among the Nations." In addition, as of December 2007, the Israelis awarded 40 individuals from Le Chambon and its environs the designation of "Righteous."*

Elzbieta Zawacka (Poland 1909 – 2009)

Elzbieta, known as 'Agent Zo' was a prominent member of the Home Army, building an intelligence network across Silesia comprised solely of 300 women within 2 months.

Elzbieta Zawacka

Her blonde hair and perfect German made her an ideal candidate to act as a courier, smuggling microfilms packed with military information hidden in objects such as toothpaste tins, keys and cigarette lighters - often into Berlin where the illicit cargo would be handed to another agent to be passed on to the West.

On one journey by train, she realised she was being followed, and jumped from the moving train to escape capture. With her cover blown, the Gestapo arrested her family and over 100 underground operatives.

Elzbieta then joined the Polish Foreign Liaison Department, responsible for communications between the Home Army and the Polish Government in Exile in London. In February 1943, she reached London after an arduous and dangerous 1,000 mile journey via France, Andorra, Spain, and Gibraltar.

In Britain she enlisted as the only female member of the Polish elite Special Forces – the 'Silent Unseen' – before parachuting back behind enemy lines into Nazi-occupied Poland. Back in Poland, Elzbieta played a leading role in the largest organised act of defiance against Nazi Germany, the Warsaw Uprising.

After the war, many resistance fighters were considered a threat by the Soviet-backed communist authorities who took power in Poland. Despite her wartime heroics, Elzbieta was arrested, tortured and sentenced to 10 years in jail!

These are just some examples of courageous resistance fighters, who risked everything to rid their countries and the world of the tyranny of Nazi Germany.

EPILOGUE: THE LEGACY OF ESPIONAGE, CODE-BREAKING AND RESISTANCE IN WORLD WAR II

As our story draws to a close, let's reflect on the part those in the secret war had to play. The story of World War II codebreakers, spies, and resistance fighters is a testament to the transformative power of information in warfare. By intercepting and decoding enemy communications, Allied forces gained critical insights into Axis strategies, allowing them to outmaneuver their opponents at pivotal moments. Operations like the breaking of Enigma and Lorenz ciphers provided the Allies with a tactical edge, turning the tide in battles like the Atlantic campaign and D-Day. Resistance movements, with the aid of spies and operatives, disrupted Axis operations from within, weakening their foothold in occupied territories.

This access to intelligence not only shortened the war but saved countless lives. Knowing when and where to strike ensured precision in Allied attacks, preventing prolonged engagements and reducing unnecessary casualties. Codebreakers like those at Bletchley Park and the OSS operatives who infiltrated enemy lines prevented countless disasters and enabled decisive victories, from the deserts of North Africa to the islands of the Pacific.

Deception played a crucial role in creating confusion and slowing Axis decision-making. Carefully crafted misinformation campaigns, like Operation Fortitude, misled German commanders, forcing them to waste time and resources chasing false threats. These acts of cunning rendered Axis forces vulnerable and undermined their ability to adapt to real Allied movements.

The lessons of World War II espionage remain relevant in today's complex world of global intelligence. The importance of collaboration, exemplified by the intelligence-sharing efforts between Britain, the United States, and other Allied nations, became the foundation for enduring partnerships like NATO. These alliances continue to rely on shared intelligence and coordinated action to safeguard international security.

As we reflect on these stories, it is vital to honor the unsung heroes—ordinary men and women who risked everything to fight in the shadows. Their courage, innovation, and resilience remind us that victory in war is often won not just on the battlefield but also through unseen acts of defiance and brilliance. Their legacy endures as a reminder of the profound impact of intelligence, resistance, and sacrifice in shaping the course of history.

Thank you for reading!

If you enjoyed this book, I would be grateful if you could share your thoughts in a review on Amazon.

If you want to read more, then you can find all my books at ***james-burrows.com*** and follow me on Instagram at ***@burrowsauthor***.

Thank you!

ABOUT THE AUTHOR

James is a military and history expert, developing an early interest in military history from stories told by his grandfathers, one of whom was a POW spending 4 years in a camp in Poland, and even his great-grandfather, who fought at the Somme.

Whether writing about WW2, Greek Mythology, Roman Emperors or Alexander the Great, James hopes to spark a healthy curiosity and love for history in today's young people.

When not working or spending time with his wife and children, James can be found walking his two beautiful black labradors in the local countryside, pondering ideas for his next book.

See more at: *james-burrows.com*

www.ingramcontent.com/pod-product-compliance
Lightning Source LLC
Chambersburg PA
CBHW072054110526
44590CB00018B/3170